The Creative Life

Books by
LUDWIG LEWISOHN

CRITICISM:
- The Modern Drama
- The Spirit of Modern German Literature
- The Poets of Modern France
- The Drama and the Stage
- The Creative Life

AUTOBIOGRAPHY:
- Up-Stream: An American Chronicle

FICTION:
- The Broken Snare (Out of Print)
- Don Juan

The
CREATIVE LIFE

LUDWIG LEWISOHN

BONI AND LIVERIGHT
Publishers   New York
M C M X X I V

KRAUS REPRINT CO.
New York
1969

LC 24-9372

Copyright, 1924, 1951, by Ludwig Lewisohn.

Reprinted by permission of Mrs. Ludwig Lewisohn
and Farrar, Straus & Giroux, Inc.
KRAUS REPRINT CO.
A U.S. Division of Kraus-Thomson Organization Limited

PRINTED IN THE UNITED STATES OF AMERICA

To

Thelma

Dass Du mich liebst macht mich mir wert....

Note

Of the contents of this volume Chapter One and the first section of Chapter Four first appeared in the Literary Review *of the* New York Evening Post *and I am much indebted to Dr. Henry Seidel Canby for the privilege of reproducing that material here. All the rest of the book was first printed in the columns of the* Nation *and I owe a debt of gratitude to Mr. Oswald Garrison Villard not only for his permission to reprint these pages but for the complete liberty of expression which, as an associate editor of the* Nation, *I have been permitted to enjoy. My best thanks are also due to Miss Marian Tyler of the* Nation *staff for her zealous and intelligent assistance in the final preparation of this volume.*

LUDWIG LEWISOHN.

CONTENTS

CHAPTER		PAGE
	PROLOGUE	11
I.	THE CREATIVE LIFE	17
II.	FORMS AND THE WORLD	27
	The Poet and His Moment	27
	The Poet and the World	31
	The Poet Explains	34
	Lift and Uplift	38
	Forms and the World	41
	The Progress of Prose	44
	"Words, Words, Words"	47
III.	THE TALE THAT IS TOLD	51
	The Changing Novel	51
	Fiction and Its Producers	54
	The Novelist Rebels	57
	Plot and Fable	61
	The Fallacy of Technique	64
	Heroes	66
	The Happy Ending	69
	The Pathos of Romance	73
	Confession and Photography	77
	Literature Flourishes	80
IV.	CREATIVE CRITICISM	85
	Tradition and Freedom	85
	Discipline and Culture	90
	The Critic and His Uses	93
	The Critic and the Artist	97
	Taste and the Man	101
	The Three Critics	104

CONTENTS

CHAPTER		PAGE
	Who Is the Critic?	109
	Academicians	112
	Critic or Reviewer	115
	Literature and Life	117
	The Critic and the Cobbler	120
	Whose Book?	123
	Variations on an Old Theme	127
V.	MASKS	131
	World, Will, and Word	131
	The Theater Once More	141
	Speaking of the Theater	145
	The Clown	149
VI.	LITERATURE AND LIFE	153
	The Paradox of Literature	153
	The Two Harmonies	157
	Dated and Dateless	160
	Conflict	163
	System and Strawberry-Crush	165
	The Market-Place	168
	On Rereading	171
	Journeying	174
	The Ways of God to Man	177
	An Everchanging Moral World	180
	The Unhappy Good	182
	The American Note	186
	The Hunt for Happiness	189
	Man and Folk	192
	Philosopher *vs.* Statesman	195
	The Cheerful Pessimist	198
	The Red Thread	201
	EPILOGUE	205
	Goethe the Critic	205
	Goethe and Ourselves	208

The Creative Life

PROLOGUE

I HAVE a very thoughtful friend who is always pointing out what seems to him a discrepancy in my activities. He says that I am a radical in my notions about life and a classicist in my notions about literature. My answer is that he is quite right, that I accept the imputation and glory in it, provided, of course, that I am permitted to define my terms.

A radical is one who insists that men shall live by the use of reason. (He means it. He does not stop using his reason when he is suddenly confronted by some particularly hoary and disreputable prejudice, taboo, superstition. It is at that point that he insists all the more on using his reason. Even at the risk of hurting some one's feelings. For by sparing this, for the moment, imaginary antagonist's feelings our radical gives that antagonist the continued privilege of spreading ruin and feeling righteous.)

A classicist is one who has accepted the teaching of the history of literature that the fundamental character of art-form is determined by the medium and the nature of man. (Art is communication. It

11

must be intelligible. Therefore it must be articulate.
There are irreducible minima of articulate intelligibility. Where these do not exist art has not yet begun to be. Gertrude Stein has not transcended the traditions of art. She has not yet reached them. *Note:* If terms and the things they stand for are to mean anything and we are to have poetry and prose then the *fundamentum differentionis* is the presence in poetry of a perceptible recurrence of similar rhythm-groups. . . . No, this is not pedantic. It is only exact.)

I am, then, a radical and a classicist. And, humble as I am, I am in amazingly good company—Plato, Euripides, Montaigne, Milton, Shelley, Goethe, Nietzsche. . . .

I knew from the beginning that I would please no one. While I was a university teacher my colleagues thought me dangerous, subversive, prone to defend the new, the revolutionary in life and letters. Now, on the other hand, my past is thrown up at me. Among dramatic critics I am thought of as academic. When I write fiction I am told that I am a licentious fellow. It is all inevitable enough; it is often amusing. There is nothing for me to do but serenely to accept the penalties of my position. For the plain truth is this: People in our time and country are not accustomed to have those who think know anything and they are even less accustomed to having one who knows try to think. The radicals have read nothing written before 1900; the university men vote the Republican ticket and walk humbly in the sight of their trustees and their God . . .

So much for my central position which I felt it more or less of a duty to define. Now for the more strictly personal, indefinable, elusive things. For criticism, too, is art. . . .

It is borne in upon me more and more that I am something of a simpleton. I can grasp everything in Plato and in the second part of "Faust." What I read there corresponds to my experience of both the soul and the world. I cannot understand even one-half of what is written in, let me say, the prose of Mrs. Virginia Woolf or the verse of Mr. D. H. Lawrence. I keep wondering whether others do or whether they don't care. When I don't want to understand I listen to music. When I read literature I insist on understanding. Do my friends deceive themselves? Or do I deceive myself into thinking they deceive themselves in order to save my vanity as a man and a critic? At all events I am more and more tempted to flee from the works of the very subtle and the neo-mystical to works that I can understand. Mr. Lawrence's poetry can drive me as far back as Pope and Horace; the new mystics— including such great writers as Jacob Wassermann— as far back as Swift and Hume. It is hopeless. I can't get away from my combination—radical and classicist.

As a simple person I should possess the immunities of my temper and my limitations. I don't. I am often told that I am too intricate and profound. Or else that I ape intricacy and profundity. In brief, I am known here and there as a vicious "highbrow." And that is always, I observe, when I say

PROLOGUE things that seem obvious and plain and incontrovertible to me. Here are some of them:

If a book or a play isn't, in the ultimate sense, a work of art—isn't the translation of first-hand experience into creative form and vision—it isn't worth reviewing.

But if it is—then it is inviolable. The critic shouldn't tinker, advise, or, in the ordinary sense, find fault. For, in that ordinary sense, a work of art has no faults. Works of art differ as faces differ in beauty, intelligence, significance. But each human face is that face. Each authentic work of art is that work of art. It has grown in its author's mind and soul as a child grows in its mother's womb. I do not wish to reduce that truth to the absurd. Nearly every truth can be so reduced. But before every work of art, however humble, I try to be passive, to discover what the author willed to do, to project. . . . I don't talk past books or plays or poems. People are constantly talking past my own books. They establish no inner contact with them. They read as they run and then tell what *they* think, what they would have done, what they would have had me do. If I have one aim as a critic it is that no author shall accuse me of that carelessness, arrogance, impertinence. If I cannot get under the skin of a work of art I leave it alone.

If I err, if I do not always follow my own counsel perfectly, it is because, as time goes on, I care less and less for art in its more abstract forms and more and more for life. I am too preoccupied to be held by anything that approaches the decorative. It is the remediable moral suffering in the world that crowds my vision—the remediable moral suffering, remediable by a little hard thinking, a little tolerance, a little more goodness, a little less righteousness. If I write a criticism it is to further that supreme end; if I write a novel it is to further the same end. Is that bad criticism and bad art? It may be because I am a bad critic and a bad artist. It is not because my method and my aim are at fault. For the same aim and method were and are the aim and the method of Isaiah and Euripides, Hauptmann and Shaw. The greatest art has always sought to lessen the evils that are under the sun. But I am only I and this city is only this city and the great choices being taken from me I have a little choice left. If that little choice is indeed all I have I do not hesitate. Shall I be a fairly accomplished æsthete or a pamphleteer? A pamphleteer, by all means. Even a pamphleteer needn't write ill. Lessing was one, Swift another.

THE CREATIVE LIFE

CHAPTER ONE

THE CREATIVE LIFE

THE Americans, young in fact or in temper, who have during these years sounded their notes of revolt or resentment, have aimed their invectives at tastes, standards, institutions, laws. Fearful of being called merely selfish—that most crushing of American retorts—they have nearly all assumed a humanitarian air and pleaded for the liberation of others when they meant their own. Each has been driven into that arena by intimate conflict and personal ache. Yet each has publicly substituted the ills of mankind for those that he has suffered and spoken of the dullness of the general life rather than of the difficulty of that life which he desired to lead.

The two problems are one. Yet our liberal American's method of approach has shown his profound subservience to the forces he seemed to be attacking so bravely, as well as his ignorance of himself. For what, in reality, he wants is just one thing: to live the creative life. He hedges, he protests, he points to the continent of Europe; he declares his countrymen to be smug, intolerant, intellectually regimented.

He dares to affront and disturb them in a hundred ways; he does not come out with the plain and literal truth. His childhood, his Sunday school, his home town are in his bones. He has not yet in any instance truly spoken out. For at the core of his consciousness is the fearful and electric truth that he cannot bring himself to utter: the creative life is not the regular life; the creative life is not the good life.

He cringes, despite his showy defiance, at the thought of what press, pulpit, and platform will have to say to that damning admission. He himself, confronted with some example of the creative life, hides his nostalgia under mild reserves and silences. He is not shocked at the abnormally heavy ear of wheat that sets a new standard of fertility, nor at the great azalea that takes the prize at a flower show. He is not shocked. No one says to the wheat or to the flower: "You have not lived the conservative life of goodness and conformity; you have broken all rules and standards and created new ones by what you are. And in becoming what you are you have taken more of the nourishment of the earth and the warmth of the sun than your share, and pressed hard, in the wreaking of your creative will, upon your inoffensive neighbors who wanted only to be good, ordinary, normal ears and blossoms. You are in all likelihood a wicked Nietzschian and a rake, and your method of fertilization will not bear the scrutiny of good citizens." Nor has he ever heard a botanist say to the blade of wheat or to the flower: "You are very fine specimens, no doubt. But look at the barren ears and the crippled blossoms. I strongly suspect they got hurt by trying to be like you. You set a bad example for the weak and the presumptuous. Let us have no more like you. Let us be normal. Good is good enough." No, our American liberal has heard no such discourse. But he has heard so often and so raspingly that he winces the sentiments inimitably summed up and expressed by a certain Municipal Court Justice, William J. A. Caffrey of New York. The learned Justice, whose name should enjoy a gay immortality, was speaking of Greenwich Village: "No amount of intellectuality is going to atone for the condition of those unconservative people. The fact that intellectuality stands out in certain quarters means nothing. What we want is a safe, sound, conservative type of the average man and woman. We have got to fight for it so that the very foundations of the old Ninth Ward will not crumble." So Sir Timothy Shelley was afraid that the very foundations of England would crumble; the scribes and Pharisees were busily anxious over those of Judea. A young Goethe in Greenwich Village would not melt the stern bosom of the earnest Caffrey. He would rumble on unabashed: "No amount of intellectuality is going to atone."

It is time that we had the courage of what is, after all, a truism: the creative will is not the will towards good, towards the preservation through conformity of the existing forms of life. It is a will that strives beyond the goodness of the day or the century towards a vision and an idea that may, when embodied in life and thought, become goodness, conformity, mere preservation in its turn, and need new saviors and insurgents to liberate mankind from stagnancy and spiritual death. For the individual goodness is enough. To conform and preserve is agreeable with his tastes and powers. For the race it is not enough. A people that crushes the creative will has only an Egyptian future and will leave as its chief monument a tomb reared by a slave.

* * * *

The creative life is not easily lived anywhere on earth. The son of a substantial citizen in Tours or Magdeburg might not fare much better than the merchant or the banker's son from Raleigh or Topeka. What that continental youth would have is the refuge of a larger minority among his countrymen who understand the nature and the conditions of the creative life. To establish such a minority among ourselves must be the function—perhaps the chief function—of the American critic. To shock Main Street may be amusing and profitable; it is not enough, and the rockets that are shot in the process keep no lasting light in the sky.

It is astonishing to observe how complete is the misunderstanding of the creative life in circles among us which one would suppose almost allied to it. The older critics and biographers disliked Poe for the irregularity of his life; the Victorian chroniclers hushed up the fact that Tennyson was a mighty drinker of port; a biographer appears who is proud to have discovered that Burns settled down towards the end of his career and preferred bad poetry to mismanagement. Who has not heard scholars and

commercial entertainers say: "So and so's work is
magnificent, but does he have to . . . ?" Why will
not these people be honest and assert roundly that
conformity, regularity, a good example are more
precious than immortal verse? That is at least an
intelligible statement. As it is, they confuse the
issue and talk nonsense of the most dangerous kind.
It was this organism—this and none other in all
the infinite possibilities of life—this creature who
was called Edgar Allan Poe that wrote "Israfel"
and "To One in Paradise." To hear the babblers in
the intellectual market places one would suppose that
Poe could have been, had he only desired it enough,
a householder and solid citizen of Richmond and
written his verses, as the phrase goes, on the side.
That is the ultimate stupidity. Art is expression;
the creative will is an experiencing will. A unique
and incomparable personality has its unique and
incomparable contact with the sum of things.
Poetry, music, philosophy are the record of that
contact. Without it they would not be. Agree, if
you must, with the learned Caffrey and declare that
beauty, music, vision do not count in comparison
with the life of "safe, sound, conservative" conformity to common modes and standards. But realize,
at least, that art is no by-product of a career spent
in building houses or selling automobiles. The
creative mind builds an experience and gives the
vision of that experience to mankind.

A false analogy is at the root of this as of so many
other evils. Art is not a profession; it differs in
kind from teaching and healing and pleading causes.

THE CREATIVE LIFE

The engineer deals in formulæ that govern concrete and steel and the actions of wheels and pulleys. He is not an engineer when he loves or rests or reads or prays. His professional functioning is not identical with all his functioning. He can be, on the side, a juror, Democrat, Mason, even a writer of agreeable amateur verse. Art is the life process in its totality. The poet, the experiencing one, is a poet at every moment, in every relation; he is the poet as lover, friend, citizen. He cannot become an average man at a feast or in a church or in a jury box. His vision is his constant self. His material is not stone or iron or market values or laws; it is love and aspiration and ecstasy. His business is with fundamentals. His absorption is in the thoughts and passions of life at its deepest. The pervasiveness of his exercise of his peculiar faculties is like that of the saint. Every moment to him is a burning moment, every hour an hour of crisis, every decision a decision between spiritual life and death. Such is the fate of the creative mind—not of pleasant versifiers or writers of popular stories, according to Professor Pitkin. And its fate is its mission. The two are like mind and matter. You can neither analyze them nor wrench them apart. When kindly friends say of the creative artist: "His work is magnificent, but did he have to rebel, wander, consort with outcasts, scorch the wings of his spirit at every wayside flame?"—let us at last have the courage to answer: "Yes, all that is flesh of his flesh and bone of his bone. He is *this* man or nothing. If you would have the fruits of his spirit you must accept that spirit as it is, or, if the phrase comforts you, as God made it." And let us have the courage of another and ultimate distinction. The kindly friends will say: "Very well. But cannot our artist, for his own sake, exercise self-control?" The answer is: he does. His life is indeed controlled by his self with an austerity and stringency of purpose that you can scarcely imagine. But what you mean is not that his self shall control his life, but that he shall first identify his self with your norms, measures, inhibitions, timidities. When you speak of self-control you mean the precise contrary. You want the creative spirit to be *you*. But can you, safe, sound, prudent, kindly, produce his works? Then, if he were you, would he not also share your silence? The vision without which we perish is his; it does not belong to your self substituted for his own. You may decide to live without the vision; you may desire to perish. But if you would see, you must accept the seer as he is.

In these reflections there is implicit the answer to other common accusations that stunt and cripple the creative life. The solid citizenry regards it as, in an ignoble sense, selfish and self-seeking. In this there is much sheer cant and not a little envy. But there is also honest dullness. The solid citizenry will do almost everything except think. It sees the artist cling to poverty, homelessness, ostracism; it sees him submit to public disdain and private rancor. It says blindly: "How selfish! Why doesn't he change for the sake of good friends and dear kinsmen?" He, meanwhile, yearns often enough for the ordinary comforts of life. But his solitariness is his appointed dwelling place. It is of the essence of his character that he believes himself to belong to the chosen. He is not free to conform; he is not free to renounce his freedom. He must serve that self of his which is the servant of a great cause. The cause is his master. He can recant and change no more than the saint dragged to the lions. His cause, work, freedom, are himself. The free, creative life at which the repressed dentist or deacon looks with the malice of envy has ecstasy but no comfort, exaltation but very few delights, splendor but no peace. The dentist or deacon would shrivel in its flame like a scrap of paper. The winds of great passions shake its inevitable cross.

* * * *

It follows that the creative spirit's service—a tarnished but necessary word—consists wholly in being himself. To seek change, conformity, to mimic the good life is, for that spirit, to betray its cause, itself, and mankind. Goethe's service to mankind was—being Goethe, Shelley's being Shelley, Whitman's being Whitman. And thus, O excellent dentist or deacon in Youngstown or Natchez, your young son who scribbles verses and consorts with tramps and will hear nothing of dentistry and dogma may but be following a law of being that transcends all that you have and are, know and believe.

The dentist or the deacon, good man, thinks that he has us now and clutches at the little word "may." The boy may be only a moody good-for-nothing. True. It takes no wiseacre from Main Street to tell us that the tragedy of the life process is its waste. Worlds perish and species; a million germs are wasted by the careless winds; a thousand dedicated lives bring forth no perfect work; many are called, few chosen. The universe we live in is this kind of a universe, not some other kind. It is not tame and safe and proper; it is wild and adventurous, and all its spiritual shores are strewn with wreckage. Yet our dentist or deacon is not asked, after all, to face these ultimate risks. His boy may be no poet or prophet. Yet for these seasons of wild idleness and moody wandering and passionate excitement, he may become, in the end, even as a simple citizen and householder, more just and wise and tolerant and happy and serene, a little more aloof from mob fury, a little less of a herd unit, a little more of a man. In a universe in which everything is a gamble the creative life is perhaps, in any form of it, the safest in the end. We should try as hard as we can to persuade our solid citizen to put a little life and money and patience on it. There are worse risks, and this one, at least, makes for salvation.

CHAPTER TWO

FORMS AND THE WORLD

THE poets have broken the old forms that muffled their living voices as with layers of felt. But the force of the original impulse is beginning to be spent; a slight weariness steals over them and they are trying to rationalize the process of which they are a part. Mr. D. H. Lawrence, one of the most gifted of the British insurgents, is the latest to announce that he has discovered the burning secret. He speaks with assurance and fervor and ends upon an inimitably youthful "Now we know!" His contribution to our knowledge may be summed up in three statements. The poetry of other periods sought to render permanent the past or the future, memory or aspiration. The new poetry expresses the "windlike transit" of the immediate and imperfect moment. This poetry, written in free verse, is "the direct utterance from the instant, whole man." We have, in brief, discovered the poetry of the present.

Even on its own ground and without any analysis this theory breaks down. When Catullus cried out "Da mi basia mille, deinde centum!", or a nameless medieval singer "Timor mortis conturbat me!" or

THE POET AND HIS MOMENT

Shelley "I fall upon the thorns of life, I bleed!", Mr. Lawrence's instant moment had spoken and life had surged "into utterance at its very well-head." But what is the instant, the immediate present in this sense? It is, evidently, the poet's field of consciousness at the creative moment. But if, at that moment, his consciousness throbs with a memory or a hope, is not that memory or hope the immediate present of his conscious mind? It is not possible, of course, to isolate any immediate present of the consciousness. But if we could tear such a moment from the accretions of the soul's past, that moment would be blank and sterile. No, into every creative impulse under its temporal aspect pours the whole past, and the poet expresses himself with all he has become throughout the intricate and impassioned years. Everything in him converges toward that creative occasion, and it is for this reason that he can lend a fleeting impulse or a passionate enchantment the energy of expression and the eternal echo that differentiate poetry from ordinary speech.

But we can get closer to theories of the new poetry by saying that they all, and Mr. Lawrence's most notably, confuse the two elements of experience and expression. In the poet's creative consciousness these two elements are blended. But they differ widely in origin and character. The lyrist's experience—the passion of Catullus, the despair of Shelley —is immediate. But his mode of expression is not. Instinctive as its practice may have become, its origin is distant and its growth was slow. The experience is unique, as his own personality is, and hence, in its essence, incommunicable. To communicate it at all, the poet must use symbols—words, images, rhythms—which are freighted as heavily as possible with what he would convey and yet intelligible to his fellow-men. From these necessities and from this central contradiction he cannot escape in free verse or in fixed. He must convert his innermost self into forms which, through the very necessity of being widely intelligible and therefore conventional, all but obliterate the flaming image that was in his soul. Between that image and his fellows he must interpose a symbol, a convention, an art.

At the core of every revolt in poetry there is one aim and only one: to simplify that art, to shift the qualities of that inevitable convention so as to shorten the distance between experience and expression and heighten the force of the poetic impact on the hearer. It follows that all revolts in poetry carry within themselves their sufficient justification, since they spring from the instinctive perception in both poets and their hearers that the dominant convention no longer mediates between them and has ceased to express anything except itself. A new convention must be established, a new agreement upon symbols of communication between the poet and his audience. And these symbols must indeed be more flexible and fluid on the one hand and more naked and incisive on the other. But symbols they remain, materials of an art of expression. They will forever fall short of the immediacy of experience and follow it haltingly and blindly at their best. However the artist labors, words will not become things, nor music passion, nor images the soul.

Thus we find that every poet lives, even while he creates, that "quick of all time" which, according to Mr. Lawrence, has but just been discovered, and that, in the matter of expression, the best we can do is to substitute one convention for another with very little certainty that the new one will be, ultimately and permanently, more serviceable than the old. We do right to deprecate the stubborn flatness of work that clings to an unmeaning and outlived mode; it is useless to deny that a great deal of free verse misses the passionate concentration of speech that makes poetry memorable and strings its visual images upon a paper thread. The substance of Mr. Oppenheim's "The Slave" was permanently expressed by Coleridge in seventeen syllables of his "Ode to France"; the streaming cranes in Sohrab and Rustum enthrall an imagination through which the careful brilliancies of Miss Amy Lowell glide like beads of glass.

The achievement and the hope of the new poetry lies neither in a confusion between experience and expression, nor in mistaking a fresh convention for an unattainable freedom. It lies in the new kinds and the new sources of experience that are ours, in the modern capacity to strip both the objective world and the soul of myth and ritual, to feel the edge of things and approach the nakedness of thought. A second-rate modern lyrist has perceptions and insights that the great poets of old either did not possess or were inhibited from uttering. Compare an Elizabethan anthology with one of contemporary verse. The advantage of mere beauty is with the old poets, that of delicacy and variety and range of substance is overwhelmingly with the new. It is the freedom of the mind and not the fancied freedom of form that will add greatness to the new poetry some day. If it has not done so yet, it is simply because no personality powerful and gifted enough has addressed itself to the task. The stage is set. A thousand heralds are blowing their horns of tin or silver. The king delays.

We do not banish poets from the Republic but try to make them over into the image of Congressmen. This is no conscious process and involves no acknowledged hostility to the arts. Only academic departments of English on the one hand and authors' leagues and guilds on the other have tended to put literature on an efficiency basis with a view to high and readily marketable production. The whole ideal is a businesslike one, and since it has the subtle but strong support of a universal public opinion the poet cuts his hair, trims his temper, and substitutes alien warnings for the monitions of his own soul. He does not resist very powerfully because the process commonly gets hold of him in youth. And the pathos of youth, for all its intermittent arrogances, is that it has not built up a philosophy to sustain and justify its impulses and is therefore timid and easily subdued. By the time poets have reached the years of discretion—often a name for ungenerous prudence and tragic self-betrayal—they are contented, as Emerson memorably pointed out long ago, "with a civil and conformed manner of living and to write poems from the fancy and at a safe distance from their own experience." They are cut to fit the world they came to help.

We knew a poet once whose noble rage no penury could repress and the genial current of whose soul no disapprobation could freeze. He was of the pure stock of the New England Brahmins, but he could never endure to ape the frosty gentility that engages confidence and insures preferment. On the campus of famous universities he walked with ragged hat and flying coat and all the fires of passion and poetry in his speaking eyes and eloquent gestures. His fellows recognized his genius and his learning. Yet they felt a little shy in the society of one so obviously explosive and untamed. His teachers granted his great qualities a little grudgingly or a little pityingly. We live in a practical world, they seemed always to be saying, and what is a high passion in the darkness of an unpolished boot or an immortal sonnet if it springs from an abstraction that makes for rudeness? Our poet's fate did not fail to pursue him as the years went on. A shaggy yet slim impressiveness replaced the wildness of his youth. But he never learned to be dapper in appearance or in mind. His intellectual vision and his enormous sensitiveness divided him more and more from the general opinions of the respectably cultivated on public and private matters. He has resisted to this day. But he has not gone unscathed. Something of spontaneity, something of clarity, something of rhythmic energy have been taken from him by a touch of patronage here, a stupid misjudgment there, the smugness of the efficient, the insulting gravity of the righteous in their own esteem. He has never been able to inhabit freely a native world of his spirit, and his later verses, magnificent as they are in their ruggedness and driving power, have a touch of violence and of turbidness due to the stress of an inner resistance which he should never have been forced to exert.

Facts and reflections like these gain a ready assent among intelligent people. But let the concrete example appear and they grow deprecatory at once. Is it, after all, they ask, necessary to be so wild and passionate and heedless? How are we to know that the fellow is a poet and not a poseur? That question is always the last. It is also the most odious. Let us be content not to know. Better that ten thousand poseurs should have their little fling and fun than that one Shelley, or one far less than Shelley, should be wounded or restrained or silenced. Can we not be liberated from this spirit of miserable thrift? "No doubt there are gifted people in your Latin Quarter," says a respectable and not unlettered lady, "but most of them there are merely queer and probably immoral." She forgets that such groups have always surrounded and sustained, nourished and eased, the "children of the fire" who can find comfort and inspiration neither at an engineers' club nor in a drawing-room, neither in the Elks' Hall nor in a grocery. We are not so chary of human material when an island is to be annexed or an oil-

THE POET AND THE WORLD

field to be exploited. Let us be content to gain a little less than the whole world for our profits and our brand of manners and opinions, and save the freshness and the vigor of the incomparable soul. Let us admit the noble madness of poets and allow for it. Our verse will be less cool and humble and diluted and more simple, sensuous, and passionate. Nor will such verse, or the poets who produce it for the groups that surround these poets, be without effect on our general life. We stand in bitter need of a glow, however faint, of the Dionysian, the unsubdued. The universe, as William James finely said, is wild as a hawk's wing.

THE POET EXPLAINS

The poet, upon being asked why he had not published a volume since 1913, spoke with a quiet certitude, with resignation, without a shadow of irritableness or wounded pride.

"All poetry," he said, "whatever its immediate substance or manner, is ultimately philosophical in the sense that it arises from a coherent vision of things. That vision may be, like Shelley's, the vision of a terrestrial and cosmic revolution. It may be, like Arthur Symons's, a reduction of Nietzsche's doctrines to a valiant and vigilant absorption in one's own desires. It must be embraced with faith and with passion. It must be the atmosphere of the spirit in which the poet works. It is neither so definite nor so tangible as in my coarse phraseology. It is terrifyingly real. A synthesis of some sort is behind all good verse. Poetry lives in a cosmos. A spiritual order is its soil.

"For several years after August, 1914, I used periodically to look over my manuscript verses. The substance of them was quite varied and the number of distinctively reflective poems was small. But the life had gone out of them. Their colors seemed to have come out of a shop, their thoughts out of a classroom. I copied them neatly and wrote over them, 'Diversions of an Idealist Before the War,' and put them away with all their empty hopes and wilted ardors. Their world of vision had collapsed like a child's balloon.

"My mere poetic faculty remained. Had I been twenty, perhaps the passions of experience would themselves have forced me into speech. For what is popularly known as inspiration is nothing but that poetic passion which experience engenders in the mind. But since I am not twenty, an inner monitor interposed with the warning that the passionate reaction from experience was perhaps, like all those other past reactions in my old verses, not a valid or permanent or permanently vital one and that these new verses, too, might wither like flowers strewn on a grave.

"The image is banal enough and contains an element of pathos that amuses me. But it has the virtue of exactness. My old cosmos was dead. There is a type of philosopher who can play in an exhilarating fashion with an entirely discontinuous world—an infinitely pluralistic universe. That is, in truth, what the imagists, too, have done. And for a while I was tempted to join them. Though a vision of the whole was gone and though emotion had become

THE POET EXPLAINS

dangerous, the mere veil of appearances remained. But I soon shrank from this mere loitering amid innumerable brilliant bits of color which are not even the colors of the phenomenal world as given, but of polished jade and agate, of the carpenter's varnish and the goldsmith's glow. I clung to the humble and the concrete. But words are not things. They are, in their own nature, interpretative, packed with intellectual and moral connotations. And these connotations now seemed to me all wrong. I had, in order to continue creative work, to build a new universe and give it a new speech. Needless to say I knew that I had neither the materials nor the power.

"There is, you will say, poetry being written. That is true. There are poets who command the folk-song note which grows out of a simple acceptance of things as common as birth and as self-sufficing as the grass. Paul Fort has that note in his brief ballads about sailors; many German and Scandinavian poets have it; Ridgeley Torrence found it when he wrote 'The Son,' which I am often tempted to consider one of the most permanent of American poems. And there are writers like Régnier and Rilke and Stefan George who built themselves long ago a world of quite pure and timeless loveliness out of the dreams of their own souls, which neither war nor hunger nor any pain of man has touched. But I cannot live in blue or russet gardens of the soul or towers of ivory and flawless gold. Then there are powerful talents who seek, like John Masefield, to override their inner difficulties by sheer bravado and speed and a show of vitality. But ultimately vitality is a matter of the mind which is more powerful than hurricanes or hunting parties. And I wonder what Masefield's narratives will seem to be in another twenty years. Or there is Vachel Lindsay who knew that he needed a synthesis and accepted one ready made which is a mixture of the crassest delusions of the crowd. He persuades us for a moment by naked vigor and a kind of splendid impudence. But when you reflect, his poetry crumbles and the empty rhythms remain.

"You will say that my criticism is acrid in proportion to my own impotence. But I love poetry far more than my own poetry and I am never tired of promoting the interests and reputation of those poets who, like Siegfried Sassoon in England and Franz Werfel in Germany and William Ellery Leonard in America, are busy building a new world of things and thoughts and speech. Only since I do not wholly share their faith I cannot reach their sources of inspiration. The historic process has destroyed more in me than it has in them. And the importance of my personal experience arises from the fact that it must be far from unique and so help to clarify much that is dark in the character of the poetical literature of this day.

"Do I, then, and the many others like me, never write? Oh, yes. The wistfulness is in our hearts. Every now and then verses form themselves despite our will. But these verses are tentative and dim and like the words of watchers for a lost dawn. They are all like a poem that was brought me the

THE POET EXPLAINS other day. It is studiously simple, yet with intrusions of an eloquence in which the writer no longer believes; its substance and form are a question, and an aspiration after both and a forlorn hope:

" 'Poets have written about lovely things,
And I could try to write about them, too.
I have seen the sea-gull float on level wings
And ocean mornings melt into the blue.

" 'Only, you see, there is this pulse of pain
That beats at every heart's core, every one's;
Stabs like an arrow straight into the brain,
Booms at your bedside like a bell of bronze,
And, though you deaden it with love or wine
Or work or travel, there's no anodyne,
None, that will stop its leaping up again.

" 'And so I have no time for dawns because
I want to reach the blood-root of that ache
And find out why it gnaws and gnaws and gnaws,
And strangle it as though it were a snake.
And if I'm through with that before I die
I'll wander with you where the sunset glows,
And watch the streaming swallows in the sky
Or rest my heart considering the rose.' "

LIFT AND UPLIFT We live in a pedestrian age. Big words are cheap, and gusts of public passion are shamelessly exploited. But the better minds are wary of emotion; they tend to be cool and aloof and to hope, indeed, that no passion of the heart and soul will ever find them in. The very poets are undeviatingly severe with themselves in this respect. One cannot imagine Mr. Carl Sandburg's voice breaking over any passage of his "Slabs" as even Pope's did over the last eloquent lines of the "Dunciad"; mosaics of color or hushed narrative are the staple of our verse; a high passion in a poet is suspect like a solecism among polished speakers; the fear of being taken for an uplifter or a "boob-bumper" is held to be the beginning of wisdom; both life and literature, among the intelligent, are driven into one corner of the brain.

Our astonishingly good new fiction illustrates the same tendency. It is ironical, coolly objective, or decorative. You will look into these massive and muscular narratives in vain for either noble passion or profound pathos. No wonder, when we consider how these excessively rare things have been soiled and cheapened and debased by the thousand scribblers who convince the crowd that any clerk and flapper are a Tristan and Iseult plus a happy ending; no wonder that Mr. Joseph Hergesheimer, writing in "Linda Condon" of love and beauty, used a shy tone and philosophic symbols and twilight. He knows that love, in the great sense, is as rare as genius. The popular magazines have bred the notion that it is as common as cheese.

It is a kind of pride and inverted reverence that produces the sobriety and apparent cynicism that mark all our better writing. Who would not fear to be mistaken for these mushy emotionalists, uplifters, love-mongers, producers of "fair women and brave men" who fill and corrupt the public mind? You tighten your lips, harden your heart, and thank God and Henry Mencken that that particular way of being a fool has passed you by. You remember

LIFT AND UP-LIFT
war enthusiasms and moral crusades. You gag. Heaven forbid that you should ever let yourself go and invite comparison with the heralds of betterment and blood. To be cool is, at least, to be seemly. If there is a silly side to you, it will get no chance.

We are all for this attitude. We find ourselves assuming it, like the protective coloring that it is, and feeling both safer and serener. But there are moments when its dryness and a sense of its essential poverty strike home. Our literature is sane and strong. It has no uplift. No, but neither has it lift. It has neither high tension nor rapture. It has speed but no flight. Yet ours is not, like the first half of the eighteenth century, honestly and through inner conviction an age "of prose and reason." We are all, in the broadest sense, romantics at heart. We yearn for rapture and, shuddering at its imitations in every market-place, close our impoverished natures. We are like a woman of taste who keeps her pearls hidden since the synthetic article has become both common and practically indistinguishable from the real.

We shall not always keep on this straight and well-swept road. The lure of the wild forests will be too much for us in the end. First one writer, then another, will go wandering off to pipe like the shepherd boy in the "Arcadia" and be afraid of seeming to be a fool no more. We must recover both rhythm and rapture, and instead of remembering the shoddy imitations remember rather that neither Milton nor Goethe paid the supposed price of either softness, intellectual confusion, or excess. We may remember, too, that even those who paid the price had their moments of compensation. We need not be like them; we can learn from them. Who wrote of the height of love: LIFT AND UP-LIFT

> "We have found all; there is no more to seek;
> All have we proved; no more is there to know;
> And time could only tutor us to eke
> Out rapture's warmth with custom's afterglow"?

It was Alfred Austin, one of the best laughed-at of the later Victorian bards. We are not yearning for Alfred Austins. But even he, unafraid of the whole range of his poetic nature, had his moment or two of vision, rapture, and impassioned wisdom. There is, to use a shamelessly shoddy and discredited word, a lesson in him

Tough-minded readers of recent poetry often complain that the verses, whether in free or regular rhythm, left no definite impression on their minds. The lyrics seemed to have no resolution and the reflective poems no point. This general sense of both emotional and intellectual vagueness comes to such readers, however, not only from recent poetry, but increasingly, too, from plays and novels—from the expressionistic drama and from that new fiction which, whether signed Kasimir Edschmid or Dorothy Richardson, is so uniform in its teasing flow toward no discoverable goal. FORMS AND THE WORLD

No æsthetic or historical considerations will, it is clear at once, explain or mend the apparent futility of this growing body of literature. It comes from a deep source—from a fundamental despair, however blithe and colorful the surface, in man's power to order the world through the operations of his intelligence. All of these artists have fled into the self. In their extreme and perverse subjectivism they have sometimes, especially the painters, persuaded themselves that they can project what eye has not seen nor ear heard and that their rhythms and patterns are indeed additions to that world of which they themselves are a part.

The attitude described here is becoming pervasive. World-weary wiseacres of the new mode will tell you over the after-dinner coffee that any form of realism is *vieux jeu*, that art is a refuge from chaos, that a dainty and fantastic pattern in line or rhythm is worth all the epics and philosophies. Well, both the inner and the outer world does look more like chaos than like anything else. The mind of man does indeed, after all these ages, seem almost to have stopped functioning. Yet in this new subjectivism lies its own defeat. These artists must themselves emerge daily from that region of supposedly abstract forms and equally abstract moods and endure hunger and love and the tough interference of things. Subjective idealism still meets from life Dr. Johnson's silly but final refutation.

The "activist" group in Germany has come to the conclusion that art cannot, after all, disregard the world. These fighting expressionists have changed the command: Project the self, into another: Wreak the self upon the world. Recreate this universe which is unworthy of us. Then there will be peace, man will be good, the visible will be the beautiful. They have written some superb lyrics. Their plays and novels are as vague and obscure as those of the non-activists.

In all this there is a misunderstanding of elementary facts, a failure to grasp elementary and necessary concepts. Form in art is an organon, an instrument, a tool. It is analogous to the syllogism in one order of things, to the plow in another. It is infinitely richer and subtler. Its function is the same: to penetrate, isolate, render intelligible substance—fragments of reality. Thus the apparently ungovernable world is to be gradually subjected to the rule of the soul and of the mind. Despair of this end is intelligible. But there is from the very nature of things no other. The most violent expressionist only projects what he has first absorbed, without which he would be empty of anything to express.

In America the danger of this tendency has so far touched our verse mainly. It is beginning, in "devastating" work like that of Mr. Ben Hecht and in eccentric periodicals edited by the would-be esoteric, to assail our prose. Its spread would not be astonishing. Those critics and writers among us who stand for form and order stand stubbornly for outworn forms and a decaying order. Hence it is the imperative task of another type of critical intelligence to point out that form and order are the necessary and eternal means whereby the creative vision masters the world but to admit at once that the search for new forms and for a new order

FORMS AND THE WORLD

is the soul of a living literature. To attempt to abstract form from substance, however, to abandon the intellect, to withdraw from the world into a falsely cloistered self is to give up not only art but that struggle to humanize both the world and life of which art is only a single, though an immortal and resplendent, phase.

THE PROGRESS OF PROSE

Twenty years ago bright youths in American colleges swore by Stevenson and discoursed on style. The art of writing seemed to them a fragile and intricate but exceedingly definite matter. They knew precisely why their master had used the word "tremendous" in a given passage and how Shakespeare and Milton had produced divine harmonies by a judicious use of the liquids and a combination of *p, v, and f*. They played the "sedulous ape" with conscious virtue and rubbed their dazzled eyes every time they beheld the pages of Professor Walter Raleigh's Byzantine treatise on their favorite subject. More learned persons than these youths recalled very seriously the exercise of the Greek rhetors and set their pupils—*haud inexperti loquimur*—the task of measuring cadences from Rabelais to Ruskin. Prose became a problem in fine mosaic or inlay workmanship. Everybody was busy and everybody was happy. They sucked the sweets even of Henry Harland and were unabashed by any memory of Swift. "There is no inventing terms of art beyond our ideas; and when our ideas are exhausted terms of art must be so too." They were thoroughly satisfied with their ideas and strove only to incrust them with blithe and happy patterns.

It was, as one recalls it, an easy and complacent time. Educated persons prided themselves on taking the young Stevenson's side in his theological quarrels with his father, but counseled reverence for the proceedings of the Fifth Street Church; they were thrilled by Kipling's "Without Benefit of Clergy" and proud that their thrill was not also a shock; they felt life to be a great adventure, preferably in the South Seas, and wore the white flower of a mild rebelliousness carefully tucked beneath their coats. Their stories alternated between tepid realism and wax-flower romance; their essays bristled with little unconventionalities that were blandly retracted in the last sentence. They sought the inevitable and unique expression for ideas and emotions that were both artificial and common. They wanted a limpid medium and generally achieved one. For their prose was quite unvexed by the smart of sensation, the roughness of things, or the rending conflicts of thought

Assuredly it was Shaw who first troubled these quiet literary waters. Stevenson had written about him in his letters. The man had to be read. Gradually he was read. Publicly it was good form to call him a clown; privately one pressed against one's bosom the sharp spears of his sentences. The dialogue of his plays, not to speak of the prefaces, was seen to be literature, to be prose. And that prose helped to kill the feeble Alexandrianism of the period. There are passages in "Man and Superman" (1903), both in the preface and the play, that have the naked speed of thought itself, the strength and resilience of fine steel, that are as careless of mere beauty and as secure in its possession as a wave of the sea. It was once more observed, however faintly, that an inner flame or sword is the best master of rhetoric. Next came Chesterton. The style of "Heretics" (1905) is itself Shavian. For it was Shaw who had changed antithesis from an agreeable device to a natural expression of cruel conflicts and rooted contradictions. Chesterton borrowed his weapons to fight his view of things, and the sensitive student of prose notes constantly today the stylistic impress of that controversy in which things and thoughts were pounded back into an anemic vocabulary and a vainly gesticulating rhythm.

The tumult of the war silenced the last echoes of Alexandrianism. A thick and meaningless or a suave and false eloquence prevailed in official places. But wherever thinking and suffering was done, prose sought to cut and cry rather than swathe and muffle. Who reads the essays of Stevenson today? Ruskin has yielded to Swift and De Quincey to Hazlitt. Rhetoric is vain and adornment an insult. Our minds, to use the strong vernacular phrase, are up against blood and hunger, injustice and reaction. A new prose is arising day by day. This prose seeks to rip the veils woven by inner and outer censorships, to pursue reality to its last hiding place and set it shivering in the tonic winds. Its practitioners are artists, too, and often conscious artists. But stylistic technique is only their means to the end of expression and expression itself a weapon rather than a decoration. They are too busy to shift bits of mosaic or carve fragments of ivory. Their sentences draw impact from thought and felicity from the breaking through of the savor of things. They remember with Remy de Gourmont that "works well thought out are invariably well written," and spend more time clarifying their minds than pondering words. This tendency has not yet culminated in any master and the new prose is in the same state as the new verse. Meanwhile one observes older men trained in other days seeking cleaner, more energetic speech and young men wholly unconscious of the decorative taste that prevailed so recently. Curious felicity and melting rhythm are gone; Mill seems closer than Pater and the harshest simplicity more comforting than an otiose charm. Iron brooms sweep clean. We dare not litter the earth with vain artifice. Exactness must be our felicity and our rhythm the rumor of the world.

It is a commonplace that long literary use wears language out, that words become like obliterated coins and cease wholly to correspond to precise things or clearly defined notions. Maupassant in his preface to "Pierre et Jean" explained the matter memorably. But long before him, even before his master Flaubert, the Romantics had, in all essentials, completed the task of refreshing the diction of literature by dropping the names of concepts and broad qualities in order to enshrine in each word something incomparable and unique.

"WORDS, WORDS, WORDS"
The process has now gone on for a hundred years. Heine and Pater and Stevenson and innumerable minors spent their lives in pursuit of the happy and precise expression, of the word that was to give the reader a little pleasurable shock by the combination of comeliness and aptness in its use and moment. All delicate fancies and subtle impressions and the faint psychical colors of our shifting moods were sought out and given just and electrical names. Many of these in time were widely disseminated; felicities once curious were no longer so; today the gleaner after the nineteenth-century masters finds only wintry stubble in his barren field.

Yet literature continues and must continue to be individualistic in its intention and tenor. Its search is still for the unique and incomparable. But old felicities are tarnished; a precision that but yesterday cut clean has lost the fineness of its edge. Hence the writer is tempted to go farther and farther afield in his need for personal expressiveness of diction and is often lost in the hopelessly bizarre and obscure. This is the cause for the eccentricities of the latest born in literature, for the jagged and violent words and sentences in the little magazines of the secessionists of the moment. To them this mode of expression is pregnant with meaning; the reader misses it without being either hostile or dull.

There is a worse danger in the situation than this. Failing to find a fresh and stinging word for that which is, several among the youngest writers have persuaded themselves that they both feel and perceive things that can be clothed in new combinations of language. They achieve the new combinations, but at the expense of truth to experience, and give us glittering paragraphs that correspond to nothing either on sea or land or in the mind of man. They, like their colleagues who discard syntax and sometimes even articulate speech, also fall into obscurity. And obscurity is the least pardonable of literary vices.

"WORDS, WORDS, WORDS"

What is the remedy for this inevitable and not at all negligible danger to literature? Perhaps it lies in subordinating, at least for a period, fineness to power, infinite delicacy to emotional impact. The strongest words have not lost their strength nor the homeliest their savor. If the writer is sure that the lash of experience has hit his flesh and that speech, unless it arise, will throttle him on the spot, such words will suffice him. If his compulsion toward his art is less than that, no iridescent subtleties gleaming from obscure or fantastically wrought pages will justify or save him. It is becoming a neglected truth that greatness or intensity of soul produces finer literature than a strange or intricate use of words, and that a starry passion will not ponder beside the barriers of expression but crash through almost before it is aware of them.

CHAPTER THREE

THE TALE THAT IS TOLD

THE novel started out by being both discursive and didactic. Fielding skipped about among his characters as he chose, admitted the irrelevant episode, and took the essayist's tone in his famous opening chapters. All the great British novelists of the Victorian period, even George Eliot, followed his method substantially. If "Henry Esmond" is an exception it is so because Thackeray's assumption of the style and tone of another age forced him to a straighter flow of narrative and a more meticulously woven texture.

THE CHANGING NOVEL

The tighter form of the novel came from France; it was perfected by Flaubert and the Goncourts; it arose from the doctrine of "impassibility," of a relentless tolerance in face of all the phenomena of life; it conquered all literature and is illustrated by masterpieces as different in tone and origin as Thomas Mann's "Buddenbrooks" and George Moore's "Esther Waters." It is still the form used by all the older novelists of high rank—by Edith Wharton and Joseph Conrad and John Galsworthy;

it is used, with changes subtle but only slight, by Sinclair Lewis; it is still aimed at, though it constantly escapes him, by Joseph Hergesheimer.

This form has notable and unique advantages. It conducts its narrative as an unbroken vision of life seen usually through a single soul; it has high coherence and corresponding sharpness of effect; its seamless continuity contributes to the all-important sustaining of the chosen key or note and renders easy and natural the unavoidable conventionalization of time and space. Again and again, even in the hands of lesser writers, it produces an enviable illusion of reality. It will always tempt the novelist; it will always be practiced. If its execution is severe the results are correspondingly grateful.

Not so many years ago one would have thought that this form had finally absorbed the whole of serious fiction. Then came Mr. H. G. Wells. He assuredly saw no more deeply into life than Flaubert or George Moore; he did see life more broadly; he saw the sharp details in whole masses of it that were like the vague shadows of clouds or mountains to them. He wanted to pack explicit sociologies into his stories. They had been content to understand and pity the world; he wanted to shatter and rebuild it. The fine, impassible, continuous form of Maupassant and James burst under the pressure of his wide and hot preoccupations. The novel became personal and discursive once more. Mr. Wells is not, we believe, a great novelist. But he drove into fiction on a cosmic chariot and reduced a finished art to an exuberant experiment.

Since then, side by side with the continuing practice of the Flaubertian form, two other major experimental forms of the novel have come into view. It is not easy to add up the fluid and changing facts of art and write down things as impudent as names and definitions. But Dorothy Richardson, Evelyn Scott, James Joyce, Waldo Frank, and many minors are experimenting with a form of novel that is guided almost wholly by drawing the subconscious into the conscious mind. To them the world of appearances is merely that; they are after the source of all things in a scarcely explored inwardness and have no doubt that all things are melted in the crucible of the psyche. Since their whole world is either within or projected from within, their type of novel, like the corresponding type of drama, may be called expressionistic.

Another experiment, scarcely noted among us despite the wide popularity of both "The World's Illusion" and "The Gooseman," has been made by Jacob Wassermann. That remarkable thinker has come to the conclusion, broadly speaking, that the operations of the analytical faculty are of evil or of no avail. As the great primitive and nameless poets of mankind projected their sense of life in the forms of myths, so, according to Wassermann, must the modern novelist do, if he would be more than a mere barren "literary man," if he would be a "creative man" and project a creative vision. Thus the hundreds of anecdotes and parables in Wassermann's books are not to be taken as transcripts from life, but as creative myths which run parallel to life and

THE CHANGING NOVEL

interpret and transcend and save it. And it is curious to observe—so pervasive are the things of the time-spirit—how an awkward and uncertain yearning toward this mythopoeic novel is haunting Mr. Sherwood Anderson and, in a vaguer way, still other writers. The novelist of today, at all events, has his choice among several very different but equally fascinating methods and the immediate future of the novel should by virtue of these varieties of expression, be both lively and fruitful.

FICTION AND ITS PRODUCERS

The profession of letters today means the writing of prose fiction. The poets live on inherited fortunes, or are connected with trade, or occupy editorial positions, or lecture on subjects ranging from polyphonic technique to the practice of psychoanalysis. Only the novelist is a serious breadwinner, and hence it is he who, like the pianist or the architect, must be aware of the problems of rivalry and competition. So in America, casting his eye over the publishers' announcements in any given season, he must be disheartened by the roaring trade driven in imported goods. He knows, too, that these announcements have a solid basis. The average British novel is not imported in sheets—that dubious and tepid honor sometimes bestowed by London on books from overseas. It is set up and manufactured in the United States. It represents a real investment. It competes. It means business.

Our American novelist need be no silly jingo to resent these large inroads upon his natural market. He knows that the world of art is eternal and universal. He quarrels with the sale and influence of masterpieces no more than he does with the shining of the stars. If his own works are masterpieces, he need not fear for them; if they are not, he will yet rejoice in a splendor beyond his reach. What does trouble him is the importation and competition of great masses of perfectly competent, perfectly honest, but, in a high and final sense, perfectly mediocre British novels. We cannot all be Fieldings and Flauberts; we cannot even be Galsworthys or Bennetts. But our American novelist wonders wistfully why we cannot, at least, be our own—well, Sheila Kaye-Smiths. He reads her sturdy tales of Sussex peasants with pleasure as a man and approval as a craftsman. He is thoroughly competent to esteem their definite but quite limited merits. Only, we have our own country folk, he cannot help reflecting, and our own novelists, and a larger chance for native products would do so much to sustain the present and fructify the future of our literature.

If he would remedy this state of affairs, our American novelist must consent to subject both his world and himself to a really severe examination. He must begin with the fundamental fact that these British novels of the second rank average a sale which justifies their importation. There is an audience for them. This audience, consciously or not, must find something in these books in which the average American novel is deficient. And, if our American novelist will keep his eye quite steadily on the object, he will find that quality to be intellectual honesty. Let him but examine a few typical American novels of the better sort and make sure. Miss Elsie Singmaster's "Basil Everman" starts out like a book by Sheila Kaye-Smith and ends like one by Archibald Marshall; Mr. Lee Wilson Dodd's "The Book of Susan" begins like a work of Somerset Maugham and continues like one by W. J. Locke. Hence these books are ultimately read in America not by the audience that supports the serious British novel, the audience which, by our premise, the self-respecting American novelist desires to capture, but by the devotees of the meretricious and the mellifluous. Our novelist of the second rank, in other words, lags intellectually behind the very people to whom he should make his appeal and has no one but himself to blame for their preference of his British colleagues.

Why should it be so? Why do nine out of every ten American novels that begin competently wilt into sodden romance or explode into tribal fireworks? Why are they not thought through honestly to the end? There are two chief reasons. The first reason springs from a widespread belief among us—a strange belief for a nation nurtured in democracy—that only the cheap and the false can sell well enough to put bread into a man's mouth and that all the people do, indeed, want to be fooled. The second reason is deeper and more ominous. All honest books, all profoundly true books, are revolutionary because they are revealing, and dangerous to the inner comfort of the unthinking because they are disillusioning. They are written from beyond the psychology of the social group, not from within it;

beyond and not within the circle of mass thinking
and mass delusion. You cannot be both a scrupulous
artist and a safe and sane citizen of Indianapolis
or Gettysburg or New Haven. You may be tolerated there; you cannot, if you have kept your artistic mind and vision quite pure, be applauded until
you are very famous or safely dead. That is the
experience of the ages; it will not alter in America
to-day. Truth and beauty are outcasts. If you want
to sit on your front porch in summer, approved by
the hardware merchant on your right and the city
treasurer on your left for your "wholesome influence"
on the young, your income, and your new motor car,
you must be content to write "red-blooded novels"
and "happiness books" and leave the practice and
the true rewards of your art to the less domesticated
spirits of an older, wiser, wilder land.

The novelist hurled his pipe on the table: "I'm
through!" He was vexed and determined to be.

His friend saw the broken-backed copy of Hamsun's "Hunger" beside the pipe and understood.
"The Comstockery has never touched you," he said
soothingly. "You've told me, in addition, that you
don't admire 'Jurgen.' Why do you cry before
you're hurt?"

For a moment the novelist looked dangerous. Then
he pulled himself together. "Mere expediency and
comfort interest me little. Furthermore, my time
would come."

"Are you going in for sex stuff?"

"I don't know," the novelist said broodingly,

"whether there's any use in talking to one who can use that phraseology at all. Do you talk about government stuff or economic stuff or philosophy stuff in that way? Yet government and economics and even philosophy are not as important, not as central to human life as sex. That relation is our glory and shame, our deepest wound and its possible healing. What you, however, my dear fellow, are thinking of is not that human relation and instinct which is at the base of myth and religion and taboo and custom and a thousand agonies of the soul. You're thinking in terms of nasty stories and provocative pictures. You've got the Comstockian psychosis yourself."

The novelist's friend grinned. "I haven't, of course. I used the popular parlance to annoy you. Get down to brass tacks. What is your personal problem?"

The novelist grew less tense. He picked up his pipe and lit it. "American fiction," he said, "is getting solider almost daily. The last two years have surpassed everyone's hopes. But I'm convinced —and not I alone—that the relations between the sexes constitute the deepest and sorest problem of American life. No one has touched that problem except, perhaps, Aikman in 'Zell' and in a vibrant but not representative fashion, Evelyn Scott in 'The Narrow House.' The great task of the American novelist to-day is to illuminate and exhaust that problem as it has shaped itself under our peculiar circumstances of soul and sense, to——"

The friend interrupted. "I agree with you and I

don't see your difficulty. You're not going in for the luscious or the fleshly. Written in your spirit the thing will pass."

The novelist seemed to shrink and collapse a little in his chair.

"The stupidity of the intelligent," he moaned. "It's appalling! The thing will pass, you say. The creative act in literature is not analogous to a milliner's trimming a hat that will sell. To have to consider what will pass or not pass with the Society for the Prevention of Vice cripples the artist *ab integro* and from within. It paralyzes his impulse, vitiates his perceptions, defiles his very sensibilities, and reduces him to the spiritual level of the imbeciles in fear of whom he must work!"

"That," said the friend, "is a flagrant overstatement."

"Oh, is it?" the novelist jeered. "Well, you've never, as I might have expected, really examined the psychical grounds of human actions, not even of your own. But let me tell you that the spiritual character of most human actions is determined, even subjectively, mark you, not by their real character or consequences, but by a social prejudgment of them which has usually been crystallized in some ugly and deprecatory name. For instance: It often happens in life that a man sees clearly that a self-regarding action will best serve all the higher values which both he and his kind uphold. But the imputation of self-regardingness, as such, induces in the acting individual a feeling of moral discomfort and constraint. It is profoundly true that, in spite of their better knowledge, men cannot as a rule act rightly in the deeper sense, but only correctly in reference to the majority, that is to say, the least intelligent, standard of their time and place. That's why all saviors are crucified. They are the few who can act rightly from within. They have an autonomous integrity of soul. Hence the mob considers them criminals. Their words are always seditious or immoral; their books are always burned by whatever hangman happens to be convenient."

"And you," the friend said, "can't, if I understand it, rise to that height."

"Exactly," the novelist said. "It isn't that I don't want to; it isn't that I care more for royalties than for righteousness. But, like most modern writers, I haven't the requisite psychical energy, aloofness, inner resilience. I write a passage that I believe to be as true as it is important. I know what will be thought of it in certain quarters. A thin psychical slime seems to creep over it right here in the quietude of my study. I no longer face it and its content alone. Between it and myself has fallen the shadow of the Comstockery, of my publisher's mingled bravado and desire to avoid trouble, of my friends' over or under interpretation of it, of—oh, of a hundred influences. Well, suppose I resist all that and obey the voice of my inner rectitude and publish. And suppose ignorance and fanaticism make their accustomed noise. I shall feel affronted and defiled in my innermost self. People will snigger and nudge each other. Pah!"

"That's weakness!"

"Of course it is. But it's a common weakness and not an ignoble one. Hence my point is: We must destroy the censorship not because it forbids books but because it corrupts souls. Until it is destroyed I would rather sell cabbages than write novels."

THE NOVELIST REBELS

Young persons who desire to adorn the popular magazines or even to add to the bookshops' piles of best-selling fiction find it precarious and slow to rely upon themselves alone. They ask advice; they throng all possible classes and lectures. Mary Roberts Rinehart, they argue, is no heaven-born genius. She must have learned her business. "What man has done," they quote in remembrance of Wells's inimitable Mr. Lewisham, "man can do!" They wipe their foreheads; they turn up their sleeves; with zeal they grab their copy of Esenwein or Pitkin.

PLOT AND FABLE

The textbooks written for their profit and edification increase monthly. The latest is the most amusing because it is the most solemn and takes in vain the name of the creative imagination. This faculty the authors propose to test and train by a new method. They give long excerpts from the famous agony column of the London *Times* and ask the aspirant to literary honors: What do you see in that? Can you reconstruct the human complications that gave rise to these appeals, cries, obscure assignations? Well, there is a plot and so a story in each. And they imply, of course, that there are a hundred stories in every newspaper, and stories, that is to say plots, in the gossip and anecdotes that float about in restaurants and hotel lobbies and smoking-rooms, barber shops and manicure parlors.

One of our Elder Critics at once "fell for" this method and doctrine. He is a great lover of ingenuity, anyhow. He proceeded to illustrate the similar methods which were used by the creative imagination of—Wilkie Collins and Charles Reade! So, to the young aspirants in question, the matter will seem as plain as it is profitable. Esenwein and Pitkin may even, for a period, be regarded as back numbers. The clipping is the thing. Slosson and Downey have discovered the great secret. For one dollar and seventy-five cents you can be a Mary Roberts Rinehart now and actually see in your mind's eye the benignant smile of Lorimer the Great.

Maybe you can. What we desire gently to point out—alas, that it needs to be done!—is that all this has no more to do with the creative imagination than the daubs of the gentry who at country fairs do "reel oil paintings" in fifteen minutes have to do with Rembrandt. The creative imagination is only puzzled and annoyed by what is flung at it from without. It must find its substance in a deep, an instinctive, almost a mystical sense. The legends that Shakespeare and Wagner used did not come to them in the guise of plots, but of visions with which their inner experience identified itself by some profound relationship that grew out of the immemorial human validity of the legends themselves. Shakespeare saw in Hamlet all that *his* soul desired to utter; Wagner experienced in and through the legend of Tristan and Isolde all the yearnings and transports of a passion as intimate and immediate as this morning's blossoms on a tree. Our Elder Critic who compares the methods put forth by Slosson and Downey to Shakespeare's borrowing of plots babbles irresponsible folly.

The modern novelist or writer of stories cannot identify himself with myth and legend. His creative imagination has but one material—experience, whether personal or vicarious. He cannot get the sense of vicarious experience from a newspaper clipping. He can get it only from faces, gestures, voices, living words. A countenance in the subway may give him a hint for a character, a trait, a mood; words overheard by accident may teach him— though even this is rare—how to mold a given bit of dialogue. In the end he can depend on nothing but his vision. The vision may be turned within or without; generally, by a paradox and miracle of the creative process, it is turned both within and without. By the light of his experience he interprets the experience of others; he knows the fates and passions of his fellows by the witness of his own heart.

Plot, in the sense of intricate incident, does not interest the creative artist at all. "Passions spin the plot;" a living creature is the best of stories and human fortunes that are to be at once profoundly concrete and profoundly representative have neither intrigue nor surprises nor physical suspense nor any of the qualities that commend a manuscript to the editors who issue checks in four figures. Let the young aspirants read Slosson and Downey in addition to Esenwein and Pitkin, but let us leave the

PLOT AND FABLE — creative imagination out of this game and trade. To talk about it will only muddle the minds of its brisk devotees.

THE FALLACY OF TECHNIQUE — A certain rot undistinguished critic is fond of proclaiming what he calls his "technical-mindedness." He has studied innumerable novels and stories and plays and analyzed the exact methods by which in each case the writer has manipulated his material and rearranged it into striking and effective shapes. Our friend's favorite dramatist is Pinero, and he has persuaded a great many people to regard that writer's theatrical dexterity as dramatic art. It is a similar theory that underlies the courses of instruction so widely given in the composition of plays and stories. Everywhere the notion obtains that effectiveness is the aim of art and technique a more or less well-defined system of methods by which such effectiveness may be attained.

This stubborn and fundamental error finds its counterpart in life. Respectable persons who have never reflected closely or suffered very keenly tell their troubled or perplexed or aspiring neighbors to "play the game" or to be "sports." They have in their minds definite notions of what effects a normal human life ought to produce in them and of the precise aspect it should wear. And to play according to the rules of the game, to take mortal events in a sporting mood, means to them the perfectly rigid technique by which their own lives are governed. They frown upon beautiful and spontaneous actions which expand or subtilize the possibilities of human experience and fear them as an elderly card-player fears innovations in his game.

But just as the preciousness of a human experience lies, subjectively, in the sense of its exquisite strangeness and uniqueness and in the added grace and wealth it lends the inner life, so its objective value for mankind, when it is made manifest by an artistic communication, depends on the inviolateness of the original character by virtue of which it introduced an unheard melody into the music of the soul. Neither life nor art is interesting or beautiful if, like games, they proceed according to fixed rules to a few poor, foreknown ends. The analogy is popular because it puts a premium on safety and sloth. Any man can play at a game. It takes genius or moral courage to break the rules and transcend the game. To be "technical-minded" in life is to play safe. Though you achieve no triumph, you court no disaster and a decent legend will gild your headstone.

The case of the "technical-minded" writer is an equally comfortable one. He needs no new or immediate experience. Nor would one help him if he came upon it. For since he would not broodingly await the form destined to project its special pang and thrill and significance, he is as well served by a blunted general emotion, a stereotyped gesture, and a common act. He can weave these into a technical pattern and produce on the stage or in the pages of a magazine an effect that will briefly please those to whom art is a little higher than bridge, a little lower than baseball. But art is not so produced. The

THE FALLACY OF TECHNIQUE

artist is one to whom all experience is revelation. His moments have depths within depths; the unique and incommunicable throng his days. In long vigils, in late bloom or tranquillity, remembered experience builds within his mind the symbols that alone can express it. To distort or rearrange experience for the sake of an external effectiveness is to him the very negation of the creative act. Liberation can obey no law but an inherent one and expression must create the rules by which it works.

HEROES

The protagonists of the most famous modern novels of American origin are a queer lot. There is hardly a safe or sane citizen, male or female, among them. These creatures of the imagination whose characters and experiences have spoken so obviously and so directly to and for millions of hearts and minds, how shabby and problematic they are, how little they seem to illustrate Mr. Stuart P. Sherman's definition of moral idealism!

The mischief started long ago. Mrs. Edith Wharton was rather recently given an honorary doctorate by Yale; nothing is more certain than that the university honored itself in the act. She has been famous so long that the Yale trustees probably forgot the kind of men and women who peopled her exquisite and unsurpassed early stories, that they forgot that dainty derelict, Lily Bart, and the scathing satire of Main Street implicit in every syllable of the story of Undine Spragg. "The House of Mirth" appeared in 1905. The definitive publication of "Sister Carrie" took place in 1908. For some years the public that had any intelligence or taste was almost exclusively absorbed in the doings of those people, from Carrie Meeber to Eugene Witla, whose behavior Professor Sherman has likened to that of the animals. What, in truth, most readers felt was that Dreiser, above all else, showed the difference between man and the animals by illustrating how the human love-life is immitigably implicated with the higher nerve-centers and thus tends to make or break the whole man.

Dreiser's protagonists were, from any safe and sane point of view, a sorry lot. There is no denying the fact. But their progeny has not improved. Carol Kennicott would have said that moral idealism was precisely what the national genius didn't show in Gopher Prairie; George F. Babbitt knew in his inmost heart that it was the "bunk" of the sort of moral idealism that was fed him that had prevented him from doing a single thing he really wanted to do in all his life! And that was what Lee Randon, the Philadelphia manufacturer who bought a doll and called it Cytherea, felt no less. He wasn't living his own life but one that had been imposed on him from without. At the same time in the prairies of Nebraska, Claude Wheeler felt something incurably external and ignoble in the life and the moral atmosphere about him and, but for the brute accident of the war, would probably have come to grief through an adventure with some Jennie Gerhardt if not with some Savina Grove.

Extreme cases, like those of Mr. John Webster, who manufactured washing-machines in Wisconsin,

may be omitted. You may avert your face from the
HEROES Greenwich Villagers so sharply etched by C. Kay
Scott in "Sinbad." The fact remains that the heroes
of the best American novels by the best American
authors are all, from a plainly conventional aspect,
no better than they should be. The national genius
as defined by Mr. Sherman does not speak through
them. There isn't one of them who, if the truth were
known, would be permitted to teach beside Mr.
Sherman in a reputable American college; even Randon made himself socially impossible by that desperate episode with Savina Grove.

But something must speak very powerfully
through these people, something that, whether it
conforms to Mr. Sherman's national genius or not,
affects profoundly hundreds of thousands of the
most intelligent and sensitive people who make up
this nation. Well, all of these characters, even the
disreputable Eugene Witla, even the heavy, fleshy,
blundering George F. Babbitt, are in some sort
dreamers and seekers. They are unhappy; they are
dissatisfied. They are all looking for a better life;
they are all looking for some kind of salvation. Perhaps *that* is moral idealism; perhaps that and not
the discipline of a narrowly interpreted national
past. And perhaps the sort of moral idealism that
these Babbitts and Randons and Witlas and Wheelers illustrate is a sort of idealism which is human
rather than national, the sort that has driven men
whom the respectables of their age and country
always held to be outcasts and even jail-birds into
strange adventures before now and whose feet it has

always set upon untraveled paths. Perhaps there is indeed a great deal of moral idealism in America. Only it is not the moral idealism of conformity and possession but the moral idealism of adventure and creation, not of the professors but of the prophets who have always denounced the Zion of their day, have never been at ease in it, have always sought to destroy and then to build anew.

HEROES

There is an old and proverbial quarrel between the public and the artist over the question: How should a story end? The matter is as stale as last week's loaf. Then why reopen it? Because no one seems consciously to understand it or to get beyond the words and the superficial emotions to the actual things involved. Even the readers of Harold Bell Wright would be a little shocked could one convey to them a full sense of precisely how their hunger for a happy ending is being fed. The serious novelist, on the other hand, is often merely morose and contemptuous. Driven in upon himself by a universal worship of sweetishness and slush—which accounts for the small sale of his works—he comes to attribute an absolute value to grime and gloom, and misses the infinite humanity and pathos of the cry for a happy ending.

THE HAPPY ENDING

The controversy is not nearly so simple as either side assumes. For, omitting the story of mere adventure or mystery, every novel does, somehow, through the larger symbolism of its concrete fable, answer the question: How shall a man be saved and be content? The author's conscious intention does not touch the fact. Every ordinary reader, whether he formulates it to himself or not, sees in every story an implied answer to that central and supreme demand. And who shall blame this common reader—an absorption in the abstract processes of art can scarcely be his—for wanting to be told how the soul can be saved and life made livable? He has neither the leisure nor the mental power to enter into the vast and complex considerations from which the scientist and the philosopher will at times derive a bleakly negative conclusion. Nor can he risk the paralyzing of his vital energy which such a conclusion would entail for him. The very great novelists have never shirked the valid humanity of the demand for a happy ending in this necessary and fundamental sense. How shall a man be saved and happy? "Be good!" is the answer of Richardson; "don't be a sneak!" is the answer of Fielding; "be a gentleman!" is the answer of Thackeray. All these answers seem quaint and pallid to-day. "Clarissa Harlowe" and "Tom Jones" and "Vanity Fair" survive through their creative energy. But to their contemporaries the authors of these books spoke from no cool height of vision; they spoke amid the heat of the conflict of life. Nor did the naturalists disregard the living requirements of their art. Their human characters forbade that. Beneath every somber and polished sentence of "Madame Bovary" pulses the almost frantic monition: "Don't be a vulgar and romantic fool!" In every novelist there lurks a savior of mankind, and it is no paradox to assert that Flaubert himself sought, by his very scorn and detachment, to increase the number of happy endings in life if not in art.

Within the past thirty-five years the problem has grown far acuter, because a happy ending has become far more difficult to achieve. No honest thinker can any longer tell his readers to be good or to be gentlemen; that is, to find happiness or salvation in conforming to external and fixed standards of conduct. For it is clear that involuntary obedience corrupts the soul and that the old codes have lost all power of bringing the will into harmony with their dictates. It follows that the protagonist of the modern novel must first find or create the values by which to save his soul and live his life; that he must, in other words, achieve a personal and unique reconciliation with the universe. The result is to make the great modern novels, from "Wilhelm Meister," prophetic of the whole matter so long ago, to "The Way of All Flesh" and "Jean-Christophe," stories of seekers and wanderers and to impose on them a more or less biographical form. Nor can the modern novelist forget that a personal reconciliation with fate involves even the most aloof spirit in some contact with the turbulent social and economic conflicts that fill his world. Hence life bursts into art at a thousand points, destroys the rounded form of serene surfaces and delicate exclusions, and strains the novelist's energy to the very utmost. Yet ever, as this process continues, the artist's own demand for a happy ending grows in urgency. He must, quite for his own sake, desire some synthesis, some certain values, some rational

THE HAPPY ENDING

interpretation of the sum of things. Thus he is at once creator and protagonist, savior and lost soul; he is the food and also the hunger that craves it. It is he himself who, in the last analysis, must want a happy ending. There are exceptions. With gaunt hollowness of tone and gloomy satisfaction Dreiser proclaims chaos. Far more characteristic of our period is Wells, who hastens feverishly from one search after reconciliation and peace to another and gives himself no time or quietude to reach a happy ending in his own mind. And supremely characteristic is Henri Barbusse who, in "Clarté," proclaims a happy ending for all mankind through the destruction of the regnant moral and economic order.

No, we have no quarrel with the happy ending. Man must have happy endings to live at all. Our quarrel is with the falsely happy ending, the "faked" happy ending, the happy ending upon unreal and impossible and childish terms. It is that sort of happy ending which, to our misfortune, the contemporary American editor has in mind. For his public is not realistic in temper; it insists on a moral illusionism whose very militancy speaks of inner decay, and desires still to be told in art that the short cut to salvation and contentment, interpreted by it as conventional behavior and money in the bank, has been found and need but be taken. Hence it comes that our poetry and our criticism are extraordinarily superior to our fiction in quality and temper. The novelists, alas, are almost helpless to effect a change. The resistance is too massive and the confusion of thought too profound. Other means must bring some doubt, some flexibility of mind, some desire to be born again and acquire a clearer vision, to the vast levels of our national life. Mr. Coningsby Dawson is sorry that he was not born in America. He made a tour of the country, and writes: "Until I undertook that tour I had the foggiest conception of the country in which I was living—a conception based on hearsay and novels which were out of date. After I had completed my tour, I found that I had made this amazing discovery—that America, as she is today, is in the main unrepresented in the fiction of her contemporary novelists." Here, then, if anywhere, is the novelist's rich and virgin soil. Yes, if he could plow it up and in toil and sweat wring a happy ending from the stubborn earth. At present he whirs across it in a motor car, peddling ointments and plasters for mutilations which he must half feign not to see.

THE HAPPY ENDING

The professional or amateur attendant upon first or second nights never sees the audience for whom plays are written; the reviewer who seeks to develop the critical or creative temper of his countrymen tends to forget the character of the people in numberless "parlors" all over the land who are arbsorbed in books which he quite rightly despises. Thus, wholly against his will, the critic becomes more and more aloof and is tempted to talk sagely in the void. He associates with the sophisticated and the lettered; he reduces even New York to a village by the exclu-

THE PATHOS OF ROMANCE

siveness of his contacts; popular plays, magazines, and books end by merely irritating him like the bad and conventional dinners which he finds so soon as he abandons the few restaurants which cater to his tastes. He regards the reading matter of his neighbors in the same spirit in which, dragged to a "banquet" by some pertinacious friend, he regards the filet of sole, the roast chicken, and the ice-cream. How can people eat the eternal and tasteless stuff and apparently enjoy it?

They can because, alas, they do like it. This is the intimate truth which our mandarin often misses. They have not risen on stepping-stones of their dead tastes to civilized variety in food. While he fidgets in vain for a bite of Camembert or even Gorgonzola with his coffee, the vanilla ice-cream slides like nectar down their innocent throats. And the reason why he is doomed to be so steadily offended by the spectacle is that he leaves to curse instead of remaining to help. He attributes such tastes to inborn stubbornness or malignity and forgets their involuntary poverty, pathos, and obedience. He sits at his desk and writes scalding reviews. Perhaps if he went out into the land preaching a gospel of freedom and beauty his successors could afford to be gentler. He himself, as things are today, might be mobbed or jailed or clapped into an asylum. But the very ferocity of such resistance would teach him to grasp the pain of the monotony and spiritual subservience in which most people live.

He should, at least, occasionally attend the fifth or tenth night of a popular play and watch, preferably from a shadowy box-seat, the close-packed faces in the stalls. Except for some quite young girl's here and there he will see no happy faces. Neither will he see many unhappy ones. Rather such as are helpless, lightless, and ineloquent. The features are unmolded by experience; the soul does not break through. He will see again and again an expression of old and long blunted discontent, of an inner irk hopeless of its own cure. And in the handsome garments and too handsome jewels he will learn to see not merely vulgar display but a pitiful attempt to substitute sterile things for vital satisfactions. Here, he will conclude, are people whose entire ethos has forbidden them to train their sensibilities, to possess adventure and romance, to so much as graze the infinite possibilities of human intercourse. They have never, he will reflect if he is not above quoting Browning to himself, "starved, feasted, despaired, been happy." They have been taught to regard experience itself as sinful and dangerous. Business and awkward dinners and noisy teas and reserve and repression and decorum and conventionality have left them with a few yards of fur, a handful of diamonds, and neither memories nor hopes in their impoverished hearts.

They do not want art because they cannot want it. Art counts upon experience, upon inner wealth, upon acute sensibilities; it counts, to use a trite phrase, upon an answering chord. It seeks to clarify and interpret experience and to intensify the consciousness of life. What consciousness of experience can "The Tyranny of Love" or "Candida" or "The

Sunken Bell" or "Evelyn Innes" or "The House of the Dead" or "Linda Condon" heighten in the broker from Washington Heights or the buyer from Kansas City? Both are "clean-cut," conservative Americans. They were once capable of all experiences and responses. But a deeply ingrained and loudly emphasized tradition has kept their lives as barren as a mass of flint. Hence what they want is not art but a day dream, not reality but frank and gross delusion, not an interpretation of life but a substitute for the lives they have never dared to live. They sit at Sheldon's "Romance" and dream themselves into a glorious folly of youth which they have never committed, rejoice in audacities they never attempted, escape into an atmosphere which good form always made them feign to despise. Had they but known the thing they would smile at its pinchbeck imitation here. But having no experience, how shall they have discrimination? They have never put the day dreams of their youth to the test of reality. Hence a representation of those crude imaginings on the printed page, the stage, or the screen, still gives them the only release they know from the crushing dullness of their lives.

Such is the pathos of the false romance that fills the world with books and plays which annoy the sophisticated. It is no failure in taste that makes these productions popular, and no educational process will provide a remedy. To have taken college courses in English will not introduce you to those vital experiences which largely make literature comprehensible. The task of the American critic has little to do with style or technique. Beauty and truth will arise spontaneously if he can only break the too rigid forms of life itself, if he can only trouble the waters of the soul.

THE PATHOS OF ROMANCE

Every now and then, in written and spoken criticism, one comes again upon the accusation addressed to all veracious art that it is photographic. It is clear that these critics and readers, whatever their acuteness and learning in other respects, have missed the experience of creation. They have, at least, not undergone that experience with any awareness of its true character. They have mistaken it for invention, which is almost the contradiction of it; they have mistaken it for detached observation in the scientific sense, a thing impossible in the life of art; they have forgotten that the most delicately made photograph gives the quantitative equivalent of that upon which the lens is turned. Neither the lens of the camera nor of the eye can omit some things and give the essence of others. That is what the creative imagination is forced to do.

CONFESSION AND PHOTOGRAPHY

It is forced to do so since it arises from pain and from the artist's strange need to identify himself with the source of his pain. It is easy and inexpensive to grow mystical on this point; it is safer to attribute the fact to laws and qualities of the mind that are yet unexplored. The fact remains and may be illustrated from a simple and popular instance. It is agreed by this time that Sinclair Lewis is something of a satirist and something of a moralist, that he dislikes the ways of many of his countrymen intensely and castigates them with something that often approaches a cold fury. Babbitt, to use the common phrase, is "on his nerves;" he has rebelled fiercely against Babbitt and Babbittry a hundred times. Yet all through the creative process, which, in the course of a longish novel, is an extensive one, Lewis identified himself with Babbitt, got a fierce and bitter joy out of that identification of his self with the self of his protagonist, lived in and with and through him as well as in and with and through his other characters, became each in turn without moral discrimination, and so liberated himself from the pain which they had made him suffer.

Art, in brief, even the most realistic in method, is confession and abbreviation. It is confession through the very nature of the creative process; it is abbreviation through the necessary space and time conditions that determine artistic processes. A controversy between two people that goes on in life for years must be set down in a few chapters or in a few scenes. Where in life millions of words were used a few thousand must suffice in art. And those few must be used in such a way as to give the essence of the innumerable ones, and yet not fade into the abstractness of symbolism, and yet retain the tang and semblance of the real. All art, in other words, is symbolic. Realistic art symbolizes by essences; romantic art, under whatever newer name, symbolizes by substituting analogous phenomena for those that had aroused the creative energy of the poet. But the former is no more photographic, no more a transcript of reality than the latter. Both seek, by different methods, to project an illusion of the object of all our searching—the ultimately real.

The ultimately real! Goethe and Turgeniev and many other great writers were accused, in their day, of slandering their friends and acquaintances by direct representation. Goethe had difficulty in calming the originals who sat for the story of Werther, Turgeniev was accused of having grossly betrayed the hospitality of the Russian squirearchy. It was the same old fallacy. The Goethes and Turgenievs by the creative imagination transform the superficially into the ultimately real, into the essential reality of art. The characters in their books transcend and essentialize the originals in nature to such an extent that interpretation has been wholly substituted for description and the writer ends by actually owing less to his angry friends and acquaintances than Shakespeare owed to the various sources of his plots. "The reality," a very great novelist writes, "which the artist uses for his purposes may be the world of his daily life, it may include his nearest and his dearest, it may cling closely to every given detail and use those details with what may seem an impassioned subservience to the stuff of life. Yet in the end there will be not only for the artists, but also for the world an unbridgeable chasm between reality and his creative structure—the difference in the very nature of the realm of reality and that of art. Thus it is well known that every true poet is to a certain extent identified with all his creatures. All the characters in a work, however hostile they may be to each other, are still emanations of the creative I, and

Goethe is at the same time Antonio and Tasso just as Turgeniev is at the same time Basarov and Paul Petrovich. In brief, it is not invention that characterizes the poet; it is 'animation'—the putting of a soul into things."

CONFESSION AND PHOTOGRAPHY

The word masterpiece when not used by reviewers in their intellectual teens is uttered with bated breath and is accompanied by the mental image of a drama or epic in verse, of great length and of considerable antiquity. That image is by no means as inept as the militantly unacademic would have us think, for the greater number of the authentic and ultimately tested masterpieces of literature are indeed of the character described. But care must be taken not to let this undoubted fact overshadow the present or blur the future. It does seem more and more that Matthew Arnold was right when he declared that imaginative prose was destined to be the characteristic art of the modern world. Once this is granted the picture changes. The academic tradition permits few even among practiced and thoughtful readers to be aware of the glories amid which they live. But to say of a book: "It's only a novel," is saying nothing at all. So is "Tom Jones;" so, after all, is the Odyssey.

LITERATURE FLOURISHES

Strip the word masterpiece of preconceptions; grant our period its characteristic mode of expression. At once it begins to glow. For it opens with Butler's "The Way of All Flesh," a work that literally made an epoch. We are all the disciples and imitators of that extraordinary sage and creator who wrote: "Someone should do for morals what that old Pecksniff Bacon has obtained the credit of having done for science." That is what every modern novelist who is worth his salt is trying, consciously or unconsciously, to do; that is the sum and substance of the great dealings of Bertrand Russell—another mighty name—with the art and science of human life. But let the philosophy go if you can—though all great literature is philosophical at core and by necessity—and still "The Way of All Flesh" remains one of the major stories in our speech.

We are a little doubtful of "Old Wives' Tale." "Clay-hanger" on rereading seemed both a little thin and a little gritty after the opening chapters. We are not at all doubtful of that astonishing and still neglected masterpiece—yes, masterpiece—called "Of Human Bondage." Somerset Maugham has written many clever and some brilliant things. His plays, novels, sketches, will be remembered because he wrote "Of Human Bondage." It is a very long book and we wish it longer. It is a bare, unadorned record of life. It is quiet, sad, rich—quiet as the earth, sad as the very core of mortality, rich as the lives and fates of men. You lose yourself in it; you are rapt by it from your personal world and fate; yet you are in the end brought more profoundly home by it to both and to the whole of man and nature and human life.

Does "The Forsyte Saga" rank below "Of Human Bondage?" The question is not a fruitful one and will be answered according to mood and temperament. It suffices that "The Forsyte Saga" too is great—great in its suaver, subtler, and less naked manner, great in breadth and richness of delineation, in wisdom and insight and unforced beauty of speech. And we should like to ruffle the inveterate praisers of time past by saying that for these three books we should gladly give up the whole of Balzac. And yet these are but three books published within a quarter of a century in a single language and of a single kind. We could go to the Continent and add the sovereign lucidity and depth of Thomas Mann, the valiant creative speech of Romain Roland, the exquisite, glowing patterns of Ricarda Huch. We could go to the drama and to lyric verse. But in the latter especially there would be obscuration and doubt.

America has produced no masterpiece that equals any of the three mentioned. It would be foolish not to admit that. But if some Charles Lamb of the future were to gather, not specimens from Elizabethan dramatists but specimens from the American novelists of our period, those specimens would have to run to many volumes and would outshine in every quality that makes great literature—except the management of verse—any conceivable selection from the Elizabethan or Jacobean playwrights. Beside Dreiser's "Death of Hurstwood" the most poignant scenes by John Ford would lose edge and pathos; the mighty quarrel between Lee and Fanny from "Cytherea" would equal in energy and vitality and truth any comparable writing of former times; Mr. Babbitt's address before the Zenith Real Estate Board would leap for comparison beyond the age of

Shakespeare to that of Swift. Yet these are but three examples where we might have cited thirty. The world seems to be disintegrating politically and economically. Literature flourishes. We are not, at least, living in an inarticulate age. There is comfort in that.

<small>LITERATURE FLOURISHES</small>

CHAPTER FOUR
CREATIVE CRITICISM

TRADITION AND FREEDOM

We are witnessing a new battle of the books. Well-armed champions take the field; armor gleams in the sunlight; now and then speeds a poisoned dart. To the natural man, who lives by his passions rather than by his reason, there is something agreeable even in this bloodless fray. The traditionalist who is busy rationalizing his emotional life is hopelessly engaged in it. The liberal, on the contrary, who is sworn to the service of reason, must recall with Bacon that "where there is so much controversy, there is many times little inquiry," and address himself steadily to the latter task.

The first object of such inquiry must be the character of the traditionalist himself. He is one in whom a set of æsthetic perceptions has become interwoven with ancestral pieties. Thus his opinions are, as Johnson put it, "so complicated with his natural affections that they cannot easily be disentangled from the heart." He loves the ivied wall, the studious cloister, the cadence of great verses heard in youth. His heart is tenacious and betrays him into believing only the familiar to be beautiful and only the customary to be true. He can sustain the harmony of his inner life only by vast exclusions. As the world grows more turbulent and surges nearer to his quiet threshold, he begins to fear for his inner security and becomes petulant and bitter. He is convinced that he stands for noble things. And subjectively he is quite right. Only, in the world of reality the noble traditions which he loves and guards have gone down to irrevocable defeat. Thus as a humanist he loves his country. "Dulce et decorum est pro patria mori." By means of a poetic tradition he excludes from his consciousness the sordidness and tyranny of the state. At crucial historic moments he, like the great leaders of his caste, Gilbert Murray and Wilamowitz-Möllendorf, thinks not of economic facts but of Latin verses and Greek examples and succumbs to the shame of hatred and intolerance. He does not see that the restraints and conformities he councils by the light of his tradition are inextricable from the false idealisms of war and slavery amid which they arose, and that the variety and unbridled multiformity he holds to be barbarous have some small chance, at least, of giving mankind both liberty and peace. He fixes his vision upon a beautiful campus or a stately ceremonial and will not yield to the aching consciousness of slum and trench. He lives in an ideal realm of images and values where the disastrous cries of the world cannot reach him, and the speech of those who seek a contact with the wild totality of things sounds harsh and strident to his ear.

In every country he is, of course, an impassioned

though decorous nationalist, eager to preserve the traditions that have shaped his people's spiritual life. In America he is hard put to it. The great voices in our brief national past are few and they do not speak on his side. Emerson understood his emotional basis and disposed of it in one sharp sentence: "Once you saw phœnixes; they are gone; the world is not therefore disenchanted." "The philosophy we want," Emerson continued, "is one of fluxions and mobility." Accordingly he declared that "the quality of the imagination is to flow and not to freeze," and that, above all, "the value of genius to us is in the veracity of its report." Nor did he spare our traditionalist in the sacred citadel of the personal life. "In this great society wide lying around us, a critical analysis would find very few spontaneous actions. It is almost all custom and gross sense." Is it not precisely this custom and gross sense that our contemporary traditionalist defends in the name of phœnixes that are gone? It is, assuredly, the spontaneous and liberating action that he dreads. Whitman, "sworn poet of every dauntless rebel the world over," will give him even smaller comfort. "He going with me leaves peace and routine behind him." Whitman's quest was the quest of naked reality "even in defeat, misconception, and imprisonment—for they too are great." At last the traditionalist turns to Mark Twain to meet an even ruder repudiation: "I think a man's first duty is to his honor. Not to his country and not to his party." And yet more cruelly: "Each person in the human race is honest in one of several ways, but no member of it is honest in all the ways required by—by what? By his own standard. Outside of that, as I look at it, there is no obligation upon him." Mark Twain, it is clear, had pierced the fallacy of selective sympathies, of living by exclusions, and had solved the problem of toleration by understanding that the truth of human action is found within the soul. It is the holding of moral absolutes, he declared, and their imposition on others that is the cause of every injustice and cruelty in the world. "Truth is good manners; manners are a fiction."

Our American traditionalist, as a matter of fact, though he is perfectly sincere, uses the names of Emerson and Whitman and Mark Twain in a slightly decorative fashion. His heart is elsewhere. It is with the Puritan tradition against which each of the three rebelled. It is with ancestral, not with insurgent voices. It is on the side of a spiritual frugality that has ended in meagerness, and of a moral code that has drained and enfeebled life. For it is not, one fears, of the heroic moment of Puritanism that he thinks, of the moment in history when Puritanism, too, was a force of liberation and revolt. That moment is embodied in the author of the "Areopagitica" and him our traditionalist in reality belittles and betrays. He appeals to the Pilgrim Fathers. And it is true that they came to find liberty for themselves. But the liberty they sought was indeed a selective ideal and included the liberty to burn witches and scourge Quakers. Bradford's name is an ominous one to which to appeal in the modern world. There were those, we are told in "New England's Memorial," who "pretended a great zeal for liberty of conscience, but endeavored to introduce such a liberty of will as would have proved prejudicial, if not destructive, to civil and church societies." And to these were added "many of that pernicious sect called Quakers, whose opinions are a composition of many errors." That has a curiously contemporary sound and flavor. It might have been written into the resolutions of defense committees or the promulgations of censors. Yet in his innermost mind our traditionalist clings to that spirit. He defends it and identifies it with the spirit of our national life. And, in a sense, it has unhappily become so. We live by Bradford rather than by Emerson and sedulously cultivate a civilization which Matthew Arnold called "the very lowest form of intelligential life which one can imagine as saving." It is our Puritan cities and countrysides that might well have wrung from him the cry: "Can any life be imagined more dismal, more hideous, more unenviable?" It is Arnold's perception that liberal American criticism shares; it is his task that we seek here to accomplish. The world has changed; the philosophical background of our effort is not quite his. But our aim is his own, the aim of "of making human life, hampered by a past it has outgrown, natural and rational."

To accomplish this aim the American spirit must be liberated for a new contact with reality. The anterior assumptions of the Puritan tradition must be broken down. The light of a free criticism must be turned on values that no longer work. The cre-

TRADITION AND FREEDOM

ative spirit in literature and life arises invariably from an immediate relation to the undistorted nature of things. No traditionalist has ever founded a tradition, though he may, like Dante, sum one up. The home of human civilization is not in any given set of forms but in the mind itself. It is the undue hardening of particular forms that threatens recurrently to destroy it. "We want a ship in these billows we inhabit!" Emerson exclaims. "An angular, dogmatic house would be rent to chips and splinters." The house has been rent. Our conservative critics huddle in its damp chambers trying to mend the roof. They have, as always in such periods, the support of the official forces of society. Yet that very fact should give the nobler of them pause. When have the forces of the world ever befriended the forces of the spirit? Meanwhile the liberal critic pursues his task. Like the modern poet he seeks, as Arnold said of Goethe, "to interpret human life afresh and to supply a new spiritual basis for it." It is not an easy task in a slothful and intolerant world; it is hard that spirits caught in a web of their own emotions should join powers with whom they have in reality nothing in common, and cast the first stone.

DISCIPLINE AND CULTURE

Those whom their friends at times and their enemies more frequently call "the younger intellectuals" have not always armored themselves either wisely or sufficiently against inevitable jibes and darts. Protesting against the painful tightness of an over-regimented society, they have been accused of wanting to run amuck; repudiating dead tradition, they have had flung at them the supposedly withering words of promiscuity and license. In these final retorts there lurks a fallacy which a schoolboy ought to be able to discover. But most of us are mere nominalists; ugly words seem to fill us with awe; they seem suddenly to rise before us like walls we cannot scale. Thus kindly and by no means stupid people have been permitted to suppose that certain blameless literary gentlemen in our midst wreck homes before breakfast and use no beverage but gin.

The popular fallacy which the younger intellectuals have not guarded against is that it is possible to act without choice simply because you are tired of one particular and monotonous choice. What the Elder Critics have, in effect, said to them is strictly analogous to this: "What, you will not eat the wholesome and manly porridge of our ancestors? No doubt you feed on babies' bones." And the readers of the conservative press echo: "They feed on babies' bones." The younger intellectuals have airily forgotten to answer: "But, dear people, there is cream of wheat and wheatena and hominy and corn-flakes and puffed rice and new things yet uninvented. It is you who are coarse; it is you who exercise no choice and are therefore promiscuous; it is we who are fastidious and selective and delicate and conscientious and austere. You speak of us as undisciplined. You do not know what discipline is. To narrow the possible choices of life is to eliminate discipline more and more. Your true conservatives are the animals whose habits know no change in a thousand generations. They practice no discipline, for they need none."

The familiar line from Wordsworth's "Ode to Duty" will make the point quite clear. "Me," wrote the poet with that inversion which now seems quainter to us than it should, "me this uncharter'd freedom tires." Now a wholly unchartered freedom is, of course, not possible to a man who is neither drunk nor mad. All sane human action is motivated and into its motivation enter not only desire but moral and æsthetic preferences, economic urges and repressions, social loves and fears. The sum of such motives is the charter of a given action. What the Elder Critics, without quite daring to say it, have meant is that there is but one charter for civilized action. Experience contradicts this flatly, and what the younger intellectuals have tried to do is to seek within experience new, more liberal, more gracious charters according to which men may live. Far from repudiating self-discipline they have insisted upon the necessity of its exercise. What they have disliked is herd-discipline masquerading as self-discipline and the mechanical adherence to charters that do not arise from the needs of the soul.

For the sources of our charters of action, for the shaping of beautiful motives, they have gone to a rational culture. For it is the precise virtue of culture that it makes for high and fastidious choice in both art and life and yet gives free play to personality and prevents the individual from lapsing into the herd unit. Thus they have, as their accusers have never tired of saying, talked a great deal about the self. They have not meant an undisciplined self; they have meant a self that draws the powers of its discipline from within, that chooses its duties, creates its charter, and thus can never lose that moral harmony and freshness of impulse without which the fairest-seeming actions have no true virtue at their core. Even as artists who survey the same scenes and actions will weave them into utterly different yet equally beautiful works, so, upon this view, the same material will be shaped into many kinds of life—all beautiful, all moral, all disciplined, each exercising its freedom according to a charter which itself has found.

DISCIPLINE AND CULTURE

The critic's character, like the poet's, has undergone many transformations in the course of time. During long ages the didactic notion of the critic prevailed, and learned and self-satisfied men cling to it still. According to this notion, which commends itself easily to superficial thinking, the critic is an expert in fixed rules by which art is to be judged. He handles standards, both moral and æsthetic, very much as a draper does his yardstick. No subtlety of learning or refinement of reasoning changes the character of the didactic critic to whose gigantic futility the history of his craft bears eloquent witness. His anterior assumptions always invalidated his judgments, and his divine yardstick turned out to be the weapon of his angry prejudices. The scientific critic, a type that flourished mightily but briefly, is both more amiable and less pretentious. But he is

THE CRITIC AND HIS USES

the victim of an analogy of deadly falseness. You can classify phenomena that are identical—moons, beetles, rocks. You cannot classify phenomena that are unique. There is no "évolution des genres" because, closely looked upon, there are no "genres." There are only individuals expressing their personal sense of life in art; and there are the imitators of these individuals who do not count.

The impressionists were fully aware of the sterility of both the didactic and the scientific methods. They sought to disengage the peculiar aroma of books and pictures and, being frankly subjective, produced many pages of beautiful creative literature. But they restricted themselves a little narrowly to æsthetic considerations and, conscious always of their reaction against the older schools, hesitated to assume the critical functions which they had seen so absurdly exercised. A gentle pessimism haunts all their books, and the elegiac sense of the passing of a world from which their own souls were not yet wholly estranged. If Sainte-Beuve wrote "the natural history of minds," the impressionists clung timidly to the history of their own minds. They paid homage to the dead rules of criticism by not daring to proceed without them beyond the autumnal gardens of their own souls.

It is at this point that the modern critic parts company with the masters whom he has loved and from whom he has learned so much. His is a hardier and a cooler nature. Skepticism does not wound his heart and the perception of change leaves him quite untroubled. He has shifted his whole point of vision and has no inner or outer need of any comfortable absolutes. For he sees art as an integral part of the life-process, as the life-process itself growing articulate through chosen personalities. That it should do so at all, that life should speak in terms of beauty—this is to him the central and sufficient fact which satisfies the "idealistic" cravings of his mind. Beauty exists—there is his heartening and transcendent truth. In beauty he admits differences of method, of growth, and degrees of intensity; he admits no moralistic qualifications of better or worse, higher or lower, through the choice of one sort of subject matter rather than another or one technique of expression rather than another. Veracity of substance and intensity of expression are his sole tests. He may privately entertain the opinion that certain kinds of subjects and certain technical methods have actually made for veracity and intensity more often than others. But he is eager to have that opinion refuted and the realm of beauty thus enlarged. He knows nothing of a beauty that is wrong or immoral. He knows, negatively, only the false or the feeble expression that misses its own inherent aim through disloyalty to experience or through failure in articulateness. Wherever deep experience attains intense expression, there is art.

This critic, like the poet, is born and can hardly be made. The reading of many books will help him little unless he has the sense of life, unless its throb comes to him even through alien speech and remote forms. No partisanship must curb his humanity, no prejudice blunt the sensitiveness of his spirit. He must be himself a seeker after beauty, after the expression that makes life luminous and rich; he must be able to identify his own self with men and things. And he must be sensitive to the general drift of the many lives that make the world, and neither expect romantic expansiveness in small and rigid societies nor the severities of classical synthesis in an age of democratic revolution. He must share imaginatively the life of other periods and very practically that of his own. The passions of its freest minds must be his also, though at the core he may always keep a touch of coolness to save his inner processes from hardening even in the best of causes. His highest aim will always be to keep his perception of the relation of literature to life firm and unclouded, lest in the ardor of his personal seeking he fall into the old error of condemning passions he does not share or opinions to which he is hostile. All life must be his province. If it is, he cannot go far wrong in his dealings with art. If he has been, directly or vicariously, a part of all human experience, the expression of no form of it can startle or befog his mind.

His function in modern society is a grave and arduous one. He must constantly reinterpret the past for the uses of the present, in order that it may contribute to the creation of that cultural atmosphere which is his final practical aim. Thus he will be both philosopher and historian. He will illustrate the continuity and oneness of art as the expression of life, and thus establish at once the validity and use of the art of his own contemporaries. This art he will be careful to interpret in relation to the vital forces from which it springs, in order that by its reaction on its audience it may serve to establish the cultural environment within which the experience of individuals can be most free and rich. None will be more acutely aware of this interaction between art and life than himself, or do more to clarify it and make it effectual. The expression of life in art reacts on life. Poets create new moods in love for their hearers; dramatists have altered the structure of society. It will be the critic's task to heighten and increase this enrichment and liberation of life. He will seek to make art, which expresses life, re-enter life through the sharpened senses of all capable of receiving its impressions. *[THE CRITIC AND HIS USES]*

The virtue of this program of the modern critic is that it translates the severest spirtual efforts into direct social action, and yet leaves him serene and detached. To free souls through the ministry of art, to create an atmosphere in which that freedom may be exercised and art itself may thrive—these are the ends for which he will unceasingly labor. The purely æsthetic has not lost its magic or its glow for him. But it needs no nursing. It will appear whenever the source of art, which is experience, is kept untrammeled, strong, and full.

The notion of a necessary connection between the critical and the creative functions has rarely been entertained in America. Our older critics and historians of literature made it a vigorous custom to mention none but the dead and gave their struggling contemporaries the barren consolation that posterity *[THE CRITIC AND THE ARTIST]* would be just. This custom was wholly derived from England. In France and Germany the danger has often been the contrary one and critical theory has, during many periods, shot beyond creative practice. Today the makers of a vigorous young literature among us turn to criticism a not unhopeful if not wholly trusting eye. They are often touchingly humble. Their very crudities and imperfections constitute a silent question. What answer do they receive?

From the group of critics which, by a strange irony, is the self-appointed guardian of the national shrine, they meet with irritated repudiation. They should not be what they are. The frank absurdity of such an attempt to stop the cosmic processes with a monkey-wrench renders it negligible. But other and wiser and more liberal voices do not often present to the poet, the novelist, the playwright, a more fruitful message. They are sympathetic, they are benignant. Their councils, however, can be summed up in the Horatian maxim to turn over the great Greek exemplars by night and by day. And they are impelled toward a certain insistence on this point because one or two of the very liberal critics to whom our younger men of letters actually turn, do not, in fact, make enough of the classics and seem themselves often at the mercy of tempestuous prejudices and perverse moods. Thus one, with all the resources of his energetic mind and athletic style, announced but the other day that poetry must always be puerile because it is neither as intellectual as prose nor as abstractly emotional as music.

The advice to turn to the classics is, clearly,

healthier and more saving than that. But it must not be given in the spirit of the rhetorician; it must not regard the classics as norms of practice but as examples of the creative spirit in action. There is the critic who is learned in the Homeric controversy and in the versification of Shakespeare as an historical test. It is not he who can make the classics seem either friendly or useful. But there is another critic who knows how, on a certain night at Tibur, the Falernian stung the palate of Horace and his friend Thaliarchus, who has shared the pang of Dante's heart when the vision of the living Beatrice Portinari had so shattered the poet that his friends feared for his life, who has caroused with the young Shakespeare and Falstaff and their friends at some gabled tavern, who has been with Goethe at Sesenheim and in Venice and has dreamed with Shelley of the liberation of mankind and worshiped Emilia Viviani at her convent gate. This critic understands how such experiences grew into the works of art that express and commemorate them. He has lived with the classics and looked into his own heart and has mastered the character of the creative process itself. It is by virtue of this knowledge that he can guide others in the transmutation of life into art, in both the freedom and the self-discipline that are involved, in the realization of their personalities through an expression that shall have a timeless accent, in the embodiment of their unique and necessary aims.

The artist, then, should be taught to live with the classics. But he should live with them in order, if possible, to become a classic in his turn. And often

THE CRITIC AND THE ARTIST

he can live with them best by imitating their example but neglecting their works. "Nous voulons la beauté nouvelle!" exclaims a remarkable young French poet. In order to be like the classics he repudiates them. To him as to them the world is new and beautiful and tragic and inexpressibly his own. This day and its experiences are his; this morning is the beginning of the world.

> Et si je danse sur les tombes
> C'est pour que la beauté du monde
> Soit neuve en moi tous les matins!

It is this living spirit of the freedom of all great and original literature that our critic will seek to communicate to his contemporaries. His understanding of it will also guide him in his opinions of work accomplished. Amid the heavy standardization of thought and taste and ethical reaction that often weighs so heavily on our national life, he will guard and direct every precious flicker of personality and never tire of driving home the force of Goethe's maxim:

> Ursprünglich eignen Sinn
> Lass dir nicht rauben!
> Woran die Menge glaubt
> Ist leicht zu glauben!

But he will never lose sight of that creative process by which alone such originality of vision can become art. There must be, not this or that form, but form; not this or that technique, but organization. For raw experience is meaningless save to him who has felt it. Art is communication. Its symbols must be both concrete and universal. It speaks for one, but its voice must reach mankind.

"If, then," the professor said, stroking his beard unquietly, "if, then, you allow no standards or certain tests by which the worth of a piece of literature can be established, how are we either to learn or to teach? What are we to study and what are we to transmit as of assured fruitfulness and value?"

"You are, if I may say so," the critic answered thoughtfully, "too proud and too humble at once. You are too proud because you are afraid to spend your time on anything except the perfect and the permanent; you are too humble because you will not let yourself realize that by the exercise of the thought and sensibilities of just such men as you the perfect and permanent is established, is, I had almost said, created."

The professor shook his head. "You go fast. Take up your two points separately. Life is short and feverish. It is not pride that forbids us spending our time on anything but the best."

"The best," the critic repeated slowly. "You work with such hard concepts. There are, I think, several kinds of best. There is, of the one kind, the Pharmaceutria of Vergil. The hexameters are beautiful and liquid beyond description. But as you hear their music you are also a little flattered and sustained in your favorite moods by knowing that it has sounded across so many centuries. You recall, too, that Macaulay thought a certain passage in the poem the loveliest and most moving in Latin poetry. And it is, indeed, charming in itself. But some of its charm is also in the very antiquity of that little lad who sighed for his sweetheart in the orchard. And is not mere antiquity in itself, quite like novelty in itself, an adventitious source of interest though, I should grant you at once, by far the nobler?

The professor smiled. "Your psychology is sound even if it is a little like prying. But I am curious to hear about your other kind of best."

"Let us suppose," the critic said, "that a novel appears with a style and form of but mediocre quality and also, so far as we can see, with little chance of being remembered for many years to come. But let us suppose, further—for it happens every year—that this novel renders and thus clarifies some vital and widespread experience of the men and women who live today so accurately and so closely that life itself is a little changed and its difficulty a little mitigated —would you not recognize there, too, a value of the best kind?"

"But what has it to do with art?" the professor asked.

"Nothing, if you limit art to a few simple gestures permanently molded. But the majority of men are not connoisseurs of such beauty. Life is, as you said, short and feverish. They do not want to die before they have learned to live."

"Are the classics barren in that respect?"

"No, but insufficient. 'Non omnia possumus omnes.' How true but how cold and general. Also, it is didactic—a maxim pronounced from without. We need experience more than maxims."

The professor shook his head. "It seems to me that we began by talking about one thing and are now talking about another. I am acquainted with the modern doctrine of art as expression. I understand it though it means little to me. On the basis of it I am not unwilling to grant you an excellence in literature made up of such elements as you have described. I still desire to know how, without norms or standards, we are to recognize among the works of this or any age those that will be permanent because their beauty will be, like the beauty of the Pharmaceutria, permanently persuasive to the souls of men."

"You want," the critic said, choosing his words carefully, "a recognition before the fact which cannot come because it is not born until after the fact. The friends of Vergil by believing in the permanence of his poem began to create it. Their equals in sensitiveness and insight approved that judgment in generation after generation. Separately these judgments were subjective and independent of external norms in every instance. Collectively, however, the agreement of so many identical subjective reactions over so long a period of time came to constitute the only kind of objectivity we know at all. I said you were too humble and I meant that you will not take toward some contemporary work the attitude that Vergil's friends took and so begin the creation of that permanence in beauty which you crave."

"But suppose I have not their good fortune and my subjective decision is reversed?"

The critic smiled. "The extremes of humility and pride are one," he said. "You are too humble to judge because you are too proud to take the chance of having judged wrongly. You want the safeguard of standards in order to avoid the risks of human fate."

"I do not admit your picture of human fate," the professor cried, "as excluding the recognizably transcendent and eternal! Where are we to rest in this mad flux?"

"We are in it," the critic said sadly. "No shore is visible. I refuse to suppose a shore because I am weary at moments. Life and art create their values from within. Here or nowhere is eternity."

The professor arose. "I refuse to live in such a world!"

The critic smiled again. "That is an old and frequent cry. Your classics have not taught you their great lesson of resignation. But that cry grants my case. I, at least, have a chance of being more useful than you who ask for a moon you do not even see."

"It is better to ask for a moon that does not exist than to consent to a moonless world."

"Ah, you idealists," the critic said, "you offer a fine and heroic spectacle for us in our leisure hours. But we who are meek do the work that needs to be done upon the earth and perhaps we shall, as it was foretold of us, inherit it after all."

The Very Young Critic was vexed. "With all possible respect," he said, "I don't see that all your talk about Plato and the consensus of mankind and the great moral tradition gets you anywhere. You wouldn't be reading Plato himself if he hadn't been such a charming writer. And in his most charming thing 'The Banquet' there are both incidents and doctrines that, well—they don't exactly fit into your scheme."

The Graybeard smiled. "I was aware that you had probably read nothing of Plato except 'The Banquet' and that probably again in the version and interpretation of Shelley. The fact remains that man is distinguished from the brutes by having built up a spiritual universe of values and traditions and ideals within this sensible world. That is the City of God in which Sophocles and Plato, Dante and Shakespeare are the rulers. There is beauty enough in that city. But that beauty is the expression of the highest aspirations of the race. To be disloyal to those aspirations is to tear down the walls of the city which noble spirits in many centuries have built against the winds of paganism and license and degradation and despair."

The Very Young Critic who limped a little when he walked had a rather flippant expression. "I notice that your walls didn't keep out the war. That was some example of degradation and despair!"

"To those who didn't grasp its purpose and meaning!" The Graybeard grew a little red in the face. "Of course, if I'm talking to a pacifist or a pro-German . . ."

"Not at all," said the Very Young Critic, "though I confess your City seemed a little queer with Goethe out of it. I'm fed up on both the war and its consequences. The whole thing seems pretty rotten. And one can't help noticing that the moral old gentlemen got us into the great mess and can't get us out. That's one big reason why I repudiate, so far as art goes, the expression of moral values. Such expression is futile. Beauty is the absolute good, a beauty that is, so far as possible, remote from the muddle of practical things. It's their concern with that muddle which ruined Shaw and Wells. An exquisite, abstract pattern is the same yesterday, today, and forever."

The Graybeard could contain himself no longer. "Young man," he said, "that's twaddle. We heard that twaddle in the nineties. Where are those twaddlers now? How did Oscar Wilde end?"

The Critic of Forty had been listening patiently. "I don't like to see you two quarreling," he said at last, "because there's no fundamental difference between you."

"Oh, isn't there though!" the Very Young Critic chirped. The Graybeard smiled his disdain.

"Why, no," said the Critic of Forty. "You're like two people in a ship. The ship is on the rocks; her bottom's fouled; her sails are rags and her masts in splinters. Most of the passengers are dead, the rest and the crew are rotten with scurvy. You two happened to be in the first cabin and happened to have private supplies. So you talk. One of you," he turned to the Graybeard, "says: 'This is the noble ship on which my fathers sailed. Their charts are as near an approach to absolute truth as man can reach. Let no one rock the boat. So long as we stick to this ship and these charts we are, at least, upholding the dignity that befits man, the traditions of our race and nation, and defeating the savagery of human nature.' And you," he grinned in the direction of the Very Young Critic, "reply: 'Well, things look bad but no doubt you're right. Let's fiddle a tune!'"

The Graybeard looked severe. "Parables and analogies are notoriously misleading. A skipper's charts may not be absolutely accurate. He'll do no better by throwing them overboard."

"It's not a question," the Critic of Forty said, "of tolerably inaccurate charts, but of such as are necessarily and demonstrably misleading. But I shall drop my analogy. To talk about a beautiful abstract pattern except in the arts of decoration is meaningless. Literature, at all events, since it deals with the actions and passions of men, must express both the values which men hold and live by and the author's attitude to those values which is, in turn, the necessary expression of his own. Hence literature can no more avoid moral and philosophical and even political and economic issues than a man can jump out of his skin."

The Graybeard looked benign. "Precisely," he said.

The Critic of Forty smiled. "Ah, but you're forgetting how I started. I agree with you that literature is practical and moral and I do not agree with our young friend, who doesn't really agree with himself, that it can be abstracted from morals and practice. But you mean one set of morals and one kind of practice. You are thinking of a set of morals long formulated and a kind of practice long agreed upon.

And you want literature to illustrate these. You want, if you'll forgive my returning to my feeble illustration, to keep on poring over the old charts while the ship goes utterly to pieces and the rest of the passengers and the crew die in agony. That's not what I want. I want literature within its own field to coöperate with both the critical and creative movement by which the human intelligence must reconstruct the moral and practical basis of life, if life is to persist at all. We have followed the old charts. We have built up institutions and enacted codes and compelled obedience. And we are on the rocks. Two-thirds of mankind is sick in body. *All* of mankind is sick in soul. And one of you says: 'Let us go on precisely as before. At least we shall be moral and dignified.' And the other says: 'Let us have an agreeable time.' As though that were to be had for the wanting. Literature must go upon a voyage of discovery. It must immerse itself in a study of human nature as human nature really is; it must be uninhibited by such catch-words as 'license,' 'savagery,' 'dignity'; it must co-operate with the reason in discovering what is fit and beautiful for such a being as man in such a world as the present. That effort, unhampered by myth and superstition and the cold touch of the dead who knew less than we, has never been attempted. It is being made today. It is being made everywhere. But the new fiction in England and, especially in America, is our best example. These writers are intensely preoccupied with morality——"

The Graybeard snorted and arose. "With immorality you mean, sir! You talk like a Bolshevik!"

The Very Young Critic smiled sunnily. "No, only like a professor."

The Critic of Forty quoted something about "pectora cæca." His older friend reflected that a gentleman's education was often wasted; his younger coolly whistled.

It must have been some schoolman, in either the mediæval or the modern sense, or else an angry philologist, who first established the dichotomy—critical, creative. The man, whoever he was, did a great deal of harm and wasted the time of unborn generations. He fixed in the mind of the public the notion that the critic is, in the words of Dr. Johnson, a barren rascal, a man who has failed at art and so takes to the business of belaboring his betters. Hence it is but natural that from time to time, up to this very moment, the critics arise and protest that they are artists in their own right, that their function is a creative one, that neither Zoilus nor Gifford is their necessary prototype.

They invent fine and sound theories to prove their point. They declare that, as poets create men, so they create poets, that they establish cosmogonies, project visions, release passions. They are wroth and plaintive by turns. In their irritation they pour out their scorn over philologists and commentators and professors. They seem never to realize that their heat is superfluous, that the simplest appeal to the history of literature, to the history of criticism proves their point.

WHO IS THE CRITIC? Perhaps they have been kept from making this appeal by what looks like a bad beginning. No one ever accused the father of criticism of verse or creative rapture. But Aristotle, we are to remember, was, like Hegel or Spencer, an encylopedic philosopher who included a theory of the arts in his system. He was not, in the deeper and narrower sense, a critic. With him must be classed all the pure æstheticians who are dedicated to a philosophical discipline and not to literature at all.

So soon as we reach the critics proper all doubt disappears. We meet Horace whose "Epistola ad Pisones" had so long and finally so unhappy an influence; we meet Dante with his great treatise on the speech of the folk; we meet the first very great, fully equipped critic of the modern world in the person of John Dryden. In the eighteenth century our proofs multiply. Boileau was an eminent poet according to the standards of his period; so was Johnson; Lessing was dramatist, epigrammatist—in the sense of the ancients—and a creator of prose; Goethe was— Goethe. In the romantic and post-romantic periods the critics are all artist natures, all "diverse and undulating," all intense and visionary. We need but think of Coleridge, Lamb, Hazlitt. The latter, the greatest of them, poured all his creative ardor into critical form and established, more than anyone else, the artistic independence of that form. Sainte Beuve was a true poet even though the "Causeries" have overshadowed the "Poèsies de Joseph Delorme," Lemaître a dramatist and writer of *contes*, Gourmont a "maker" in every field. If we must omit

Brunetière, more scholastic philosopher than critic anyway, we are rewarded by the names of Matthew Arnold, who will some day, perhaps, seem the most lasting of the Victorian poets, of Walter Pater, that arduous artist in prose who wrote the "Imaginary Portraits" and "Marius the Epicurean," of quite minor contemporaries, such as Edmund Gosse, whose verse is as felicitous as their critical prose. If we desired merely to multiply names, there are Lowell and Poe, Andrew Lang and Austin Dobson; there is an overshadowing one that we have reserved for the last—the name of Anatole France.

It is evident, then, that criticism, like the lyric, the play, the novel, is one of the various forms through which the creative temper communicates its sense "of man, of nature, and of human life." Its mood is often more cerebral than the moods of the other forms. But even that is often more apparent than real, and there are passages in Hazlitt and Heine, Pater and Lemaître that are as impassioned as a lyric and as stirring as a drama, without ever abandoning the true movement and method of critical form. We suspect, indeed, that the cry, criticism is not creation, has come in the past and comes in the present chiefly from critics who are not critics at all, from annotators of textbooks, academic *feuilletonistes* in newspapers and popular magazines, from all those who, in the rude Carlylean phrase, have no "fire in their belly," and are anxious to make that lack a note of excellence in themselves and a mark of the craft to which they pretend.

ACADEMICIANS All our best writers jeer at the academicians. The pedagogue and scholar—alas that the two are nearly always convertible terms—must by this time be inured to contumely. Perhaps he bears it with a grin; perhaps he bears it with indignation. It is certain that he has, so far, not spoken very articulately in his own defense. At meetings of scholars the matter is either not discussed, or else the scholars seek escape by trying to evade their own characteristic function and calling, and merge into the universally respected realms of the practical and the efficient.

One must not be severe on them. The proper defense of learning is a difficult one in America today. Even before the war the holders of notable professorships, especially in the humanities, in history, literature, and philosophy, gained an unfortunate distinction. They defended the obviously outworn, celebrated the shoddy, closed their minds to the living humanities that were being reborn in the world about them. During the war there was here, as elsewhere, scarcely one saving voice among their ranks. Professors of German repudiated Goethe; professors of philosophy suddenly discovered that Kant was a vicious fellow; philologists were almost tempted to rename Grimm's law on the principle which, for some years, turned sauerkraut into Liberty Cabbage.

Today, then, the scholar has no friend. The liberal literati jeer, the really progressive students snicker, the public rests more firmly in its old, inane contempt. It is time for a protest, however gentle, to be raised; it is time for a reconsideration of the matter. Permanent and precious values are at stake.

They, like all others, have been contaminated by the world, by ugly passions, by loud prejudices and sordid ambitions. They remain in their essential nature uninvalidated. Merely to sneer at pedagogues and dryasdusts is dangerous; it is dangerous to youth; it is in the last analysis dangerous to those living representatives of the humanities who have done it most.

Not all professors are hundred-percenters, not all professors are academic overlords. There are the academic helots—helots against their will and vision, helots through the weaknesses bred of their very strength. In every seat of learning there are those who love learning, who do pass their lives of poverty and renunciation of the world in study and reflection, who are in truth what they are meant to be, the memory of the race. Where are their fruits? it will be asked. These men are not often highly articulate; their products, "pickled away," in the words of a university wit, in the technical journals, do not make very alluring reading. Between "Babbitt" and the last book of Lytton Strachey it is not easy to become absorbed in a laboriously written article on the Old English Riddles, or variants on the last mystery transcribed in Paris, or an investigation of the relation of the pseudo-Vergilian poems to the style and temper of the poet's authentic works.

It is not easy. But if you closely consider these ill-written and perhaps dull pages, there arises the vision of lives that are austere and not ignoble, that the world has always needed and will always need, lives that are profitable to the salvation of us all.

ACADEMICIANS
The scholar's study is shabby; his books are many, but there is no pomp of binding or of first editions; his table is in disorder; his papers are stained by the ashes of his pipe; there is a rag rug on the floor and the poor man has to sneak out now and then to "tend" the furnace so that his wife and children do not take cold. And yet, unless his salary is quite too pitifully small, he is usually a very cheerful mortal. Business does not allure him, nor common pleasures. He does not lust after power; he is neither epicure nor æsthete; the glories of this world seem little and remote to him. He loves truth so far as his vision can grasp it; he loves the ripe and permanent things in literature and thought; he seeks to add, however humbly, to the history and understanding of them. Yes, he tends to grow narrow, to love the "Æneid" less and his contribution to Vergilian exegesis more. Well, he is human. He doesn't hustle or boost; he is against the forces of bigness and jazz, against the temptation of mere actuality, immediacy, speed, and glitter. By all means let us scorn as loudly as we please the presidents and deans and glossy masters of the academic mart, and laugh out of countenance, if we can, the fashionable professors who praise seventh-rate uplift literature in the popular magazines. But let us not forget the shabby fellow with grizzled hair and slightly stooping shoulders and slightly reeking pipe who spends his life with things beautiful and worthy of the mind of man, who, even while he is chatting with you, is seeing Chaucer on a summer's day or has just discovered precisely

why, one rainy day at Tibur, Horace broke off in the middle of a verse, or is aglow with a new explanation—suggested, by Heaven, in neither Smelfungus nor Oberwellinghausen—of a strangely obscure passage toward the end of "Beowulf."

<small>ACADEMICIANS</small>

The learned who insist on being severely judicious even in their sprightly moods assure us that a reviewer of books can never be a critic. The reason they give is not new. It is an academic commonplace; it has been promulgated as an axiom in a hundred classrooms and seminars. The reviewer, we are assured, cannot be a critic because the subject of his comment is the immediate and contemporary. Once more we are regaled with the quotation that the criticism of our contemporaries is only conversation and instructed that the entire history of the critic's craft bears out the argument to the utter rout of the reviewer.

<small>CRITIC OR REVIEWER</small>

But does it? Or are we facing a slightly petrified tradition? There are, at least, examples to give us pause. The judgment of contemporaries has not always been absurd nor has the perspective of time always saved mighty critics from terrible blunders. Take Ben Jonson on Shakespeare. Combine the two aspects of his judgment, the "would he had blotted a thousand" with "he was not of an age but for all time." Is that not sovereign and final—far more so than either the "inspired barbarian" theory of the Age of Reason or the undiscriminating idolatry of the Romantics? No one has bettered Goethe's estimate of Schiller; Johnson was far sounder on

<small>CRITIC OR REVIEWER</small>

Pope than on Milton; Matthew Arnold was magnificent on Wordsworth whom he had known in the flesh and inconceivably mistaken on Shelley who died in the year of his birth. Jules Lemaître's "Les Contemporains" and Remy de Gourmont's "Livre des Masques" have all the marks of authentic criticism and permanent literature; even the severe and academic Brunetière wrote, not ineffectually or foolishly, on the novelists of his day.

But is there not, the academicians will ask—in the departments of English they will be thinking of Cowley, the stock or classical example—is there not an inevitable tendency to overestimate contemporary work? The answer will depend on the precise meaning of the word overestimate. We are undoubtedly tempted to mistake immediate values for eternal ones and the virtues of actuality for those of permanence. But these immediate and actual values and virtues are intensely real ones, a truth which the academic critic will not grasp. It is, for instance, highly questionable whether the writings of, let us say, Mr. Sherwood Anderson have the rich universality of appeal and the permanent preciousness of speech that must characterize the humblest classic. What is not questionable is that he expresses—expresses at times by his very dumbness—a mood, attitude, yearning, that are of the highest actuality and importance to this moment in the spiritual history of America. He may not speak to the twenty-first century; he speaks to and for last year and this and the next. He speaks for a certain civilization in certain moods as, to compare smaller things to greater, Tennyson spoke for certain years and moods in the religious history of the English people. Those moods are gone. The stature of the poet assumes truer proportions. But those years and moods were. We must understand them to understand what followed.

<small>CRITIC OR REVIEWER</small>

There is no reason why the intelligent reviewer of the latest books may not be a critic in the finest sense by keeping the distinction between temporary and permanent values clearly in his consciousness. Literature is more than a game, and the academic diversion of arranging dead writers in correct hierarchies of rank is the most negligible department of criticism. The reviewer who, because he has experienced it deeply, can show his readers persuasively and eloquently how a given contemporary work expresses, interprets, clarifies that life which we are all trying to live and make more rational and beautiful, is exercising a more fruitful critical function than the learned academician who balances weightily the claims of Milton, Wordsworth, Shelley to the second place in the roll of British poets. If our reviewer of a contemporary work thinks that, in addition to its immediate and vital appeal and significance, it has the qualities of permanence too, he is, at worst, making a mistake that time is sure to right. At best he may be another Ben Jonson saying the final words early instead of late.

A distinguished critic has justly and acutely analyzed the attitudes toward life that form the background of much recent literature. He sums these

<small>LITERATURE AND LIFE</small>

up very tellingly and declares that the world which these authors see is "chaotic, incoherent, meaningless," a scene of "moral confusion." To mere hopelessness of there being any intelligible world, to mere jumble and a sort of brazen pride in it, he ascribes the welter of concrete fact that is poured forth, the uncritical and almost unselective heaping of detail upon detail, the shamelessness which characterizes James Joyce's "Ulysses" and sundry related works. He admits, of course, that if the world seems merely chaos to an artist it is his right and his business to communicate the sense of chaos through his works; for himself he clings—here we are quite at one with him—to the eternal value of "self-control" (this term we should want rather rigidly defined), "clear thinking," and the eager search for "delight and beauty."

We have here a rough description of two attitudes: that of the more or less expressionistic artist; and that of the humanist critic who deplores the present state of literature but will not permit himself to be illiberal toward it, who is a good deal of a Pyrrhonist himself but longs a little for the fleshpots of certitude and order.

There is, we think, a third attitude, more fruitful, more hopeful than either of these. This attitude is still to be found behind many of those works of the day, in several languages, which have not gone to the paralyzing extremes of expressionistic technique. This third attitude is an old and very simple one. It is one of neither affirmation nor negation; it is one of inquiry. It is allied to the attitude of the scientist who marshals his great array of facts, of data, neither to show that they have no meaning, nor, if he is a true scientist, to prove that they have some particular meaning which gives him an emotional "kick," but to find out precisely what their meaning is.

It requires but the briefest reflection to show that the "moral confusion" of our world is largely due to a failure to apply that attitude of inquiry. Question any contemporary on a difficult and intricate matter of human conduct, and he will either give you a meaningless answer, i.e., he will fling at you a moral fiction which he believes no more than you, but which saves him the trouble of being either thoughtful or just, or else he will throw up his hands in utter helplessness, in utter refusal to rush in where the fools trample with their iron heels.

Now it seems that the virtue of the literature which, though the name has become discredited, is still naturalistic in temper and method, is that it did and does approach the moral world in a spirit of free inquiry, that it neither pretends to know the road to salvation and order nor to deny the existence of one, but is very earnestly in quest of it. Such a work as Theodore Dreiser's "The 'Genius,'" for instance, despite the desperate banality and meanness of a hundred passages, does, through its massive, faithful, broodingly absorbed, agonizedly seen record of certain central and moving facts concerning human life, widen the boundaries of true experience, deepen the perception of familiar things, approach the disorganized world of conduct in a

LITERATURE AND LIFE

way of wondering hope and serious questioning. The naturalist, in brief, asks: What shall we do to be saved in such a world as this? In such a world as this, be it observed, man being what he is. And the first step is, obviously, to show us what the world is actually like, and what forms human conduct, conditioned in the essential nature of man, does actually take. In some such manner the heaping up of detail, the huge pouring forth of the concrete in recent literature, is to be both explained and justified. We have not yet reached the stage of interpretation; we cannot yet build up an intelligible world. We shall not reach that stage for years, perhaps not for generations. Salvation is far off. But again the analogy of the sciences should help us. In regard to morals we are still in what might be called the alchemistic and astrological age. We are still in the grip of fiction and superstition. We must have patience and bear with the artists who give us facts and confessions, in order that some day the age of chemistry and astronomy may dawn upon that world of conduct and spiritual values which is the supreme concern of us all.

THE CRITIC AND THE COBBLER

"Yes," said the critic, "literature is the expression of life; life grown articulate; life's highest form. I have said it a hundred times. I shall go on saying it. It is true; it must be true. Metaphysically and practically it is not to be doubted. And yet. . . . Yes, I have moments of doubt and of dismay; I have hours when I can no longer integrate literature with the general life of man, when it sinks to the level of an amusement, when the artist takes on, as Stevenson said long ago, the aspect of a prostitute—of one who lives by merely furnishing pleasure.

"Why? Look through that grimy little window into the cobbler's shop. The cobbler, an Italian with a grave, massive Roman head, sits, awl in hand, bent over a disreputable-looking shoe. There is no droop in his bending; the man's spirit is erect. He is poor. He lives on polenta and black bread and onions. He is fifty. There is no vista or vision in his life. He is a realist by temper and doesn't befool himself with dreams. His wife, a gaunt, fiery-eyed slattern, stands in the background. The man's fate is fixed. Very well. Let a poet look in at that window and grasp imaginatively the cobbler's past and present outlook. The poet knows that, given such a life for himself, he would rebel, get drunk, fill the air with the beauty of the wailing of his immedicable disappointment at mortality. And that wail would nowadays—when the 'maker' is a 'maker' of imaginative narrative—go through several editions and the poet would be dining comfortably at the Brevoort and shuddering at the supreme misery of the common lot of man.

"The stern fact remains that the cobbler is not a poet. I don't say that he's happy. I do say that he practices a dignified and even a cheerful acceptance of the common lot. There is no use in denying it or sophisticating it. For did he and his kind not do so the world would be in flames within the hour. He has, he must have, sources of content and human dignity to draw on that the poet lacks. In those sources lies the explanation of the meaning of life at its broadest. And those sources are hidden from poet, critic, philosopher, from all the tribe whose nerves are stung by the necessity of change even if it be pain, whose minds are driven by the hunger for eternity.

"The doubt comes often and persists. I look out of the windows of a train and see ineffably mean towns scattered along miry roads. The shapeless houses are painted, as though by a cruel ironist, in comfortless browns and poisonous yellows. The shabby men and aproned women are not singing with joy. But they are not dispirited, nor hopeless, nor anything that the poet would be were he to share their fate. Something sustains them. It is not, in our sense, beauty or adventure; it is not ease; it is certainly not hope. Their fate, like the cobbler's, is fixed. What is it? What is it? There is the secret of life.

"Very well. I can't, in those hours of doubt, help pursuing such reflections. I see the 'happy well-fed drummers.' You remember Whitman's phrase. He must have had an inkling of the great secret. I see the rosy, stout business men with Elk insignia on their portly paunches. Yes, and I wonder whether doubt and the sense of insufficiency did ever strike upon George F. Babbitt, or if Sinclair Lewis did not, with infinite restraint of manner and documentation of fact, merely infuse into Babbitt the minimum of yearning and awakening that he, put in Babbitt's place, can conceive himself to have felt. And I can't help wondering whether Lee Randon isn't merely Joseph Hergesheimer disporting his pangs under the guise of the Philadelphia manufacturer, and whether Claude Wheeler, had he not died in France, would not now be a gentle but quite convinced member of the American Legion.

"You say it's absurd. I hope so. What gives me pause is the patience of men. Through all ages they have been patient, from our point of view. They are not, like poets, an irritable race. That is why they really dislike the poets and often enough crucify these troublesome fellows who will not let well enough alone and succeed occasionally in setting fire to the minds of their sons and the hearts of their daughters. Quiet is best if you can get nothing in exchange for it but disquiet. The poet does not know the secret by which common men live. He had better leave them alone.

"Am I blaspheming all I am and stand for?" The critic smiled ruefully. "It doesn't matter. It is always healthy, if only as an exercise, to tell all sides of the truth that are revealed to you. I shall go ahead upon my appointed errands and do my appointed work. But the voice of that doubt will be heard again. It is only a still, small voice. It cannot quite be silenced."

The author looked unhappy. On the face of the editor he saw a delicate dismay. And he feared that dismay. For he couldn't, in his weaker moments, withdraw himself from a sense of humiliation that came to him from his friend's enormous intellectual distinction. He knew that his speech was going to be feeble, and it was. "In other words," he said, "I strike you, in this particular book, as having played the spiritual rough-neck."

The editor's smile was a perfectly sincere protest. "You've made the wrong gesture. Let's call it that. There are moments of querulousness. Your emotions are too contemporary with the facts. Wait. Remove all you record under some eternal aspect. Then rewrite."

Certain passages floated into the author's memory and seemed incredibly raw and awkward. They suddenly tormented him. He hastened, as though he were expiating them, to admit, "No doubt you are right. No doubt."

But he felt impelled to watch his friend with an almost visionary watchfulness. It was an oval face that he saw, a subtle and very sensitive face—a face that had dropped a veil of worldliness over its sensitiveness. He rejected the word worldliness at once. Rather it was a veil woven of exquisite good sense, of measured thoughts, of beautiful gestures. The author, who is humble, thought: Ah, to be like that. Then a question leaped up in him. But is my friend like that? A sudden clearness was in his brain. He spoke, and with a new assurance.

"I'm inclined to withdraw all I've admitted. You want me, dear friend, to write—to have written, not the book I have written, not even the book you would now have written concerning the same experiences, but the book you would have written if you had completely achieved that inner transformation of yourself at which, in the light of definitely embraced theories of human wisdom and decorum, you are working. You want my book to be the book your ideal of yourself would have made of the material in question."

The fine subtlety of the editor's smile was a little troubled. The author went on.

"You dislike in my book things that remind you of what you once disliked in yourself and have now subdued if not conquered."

The editor nodded. "It isn't as simple as that. It's a good deal more intricate. But suppose I grant you that. Isn't it, things being what they are, a pretty valid ground of criticism?"

"Yes and no," the author said. "You project your subjectivity too far into my book. You were rightly tempted to do that because there are strong elements in our characters and experience. But—here comes the break—you have confronted these elements and this experience in one way, I in another. You have escaped from both into certain refuges. These are, if you will forgive me for being so crude, a graceful figure, the perfectly genuine air, and the worldly circumstances of an aristocrat. I have none of these refuges. I am not sure that it is good for one to have them. To me and to my book clings something of grossness, of violence. But they are the grossness and the violence of humanity when unshielded by accidental and temporary screens. I am vulgar as human pain is vulgar. A wounded man is not a dignified spectacle. I am as indecorous as passion and as rowdy as sudden death."

WHOSE BOOK?

The editor had grown grave. "Very well. Let those half-truths stand. I am thinking of your interests as an artist. Permanent literature is made when life is translated into the terms that are proper to art, when the rhythm of your narrative obeys the harmony of beauty, when the common is transmuted into the significant, and the irritations of the hour into the passions of eternity."

The author shook his head. "It may be so, though I doubt it. But I am not concerned enough to argue. The ground is burning under my feet. The noblest, the most philosophical æstheticism is a tinkling cymbal to me today. I don't particularly care whether my book is either beautiful or permanent, whether it exhibits me in a favorable or unfavorable light. I want it to trouble people, to arouse them, to sting them. I want it to make for action and for change. If it influences life in a given direction by one hair's-breadth, it does not matter if I am misunderstood in hostile quarters and the book forgotten after a few months or years. I am more concerned for the book as fertilizer upon the fields of civilization than as art."

A slow, fine smile came over the editor's face. "How you exaggerate. You are primarily an artist. And you're trying to run away from yourself because life is not to your liking. Only I don't think you ought to run to the cover of propaganda.

The author laughed. "Precisely as I don't think you ought to run to the cover of mere beauty and of distinction at any cost. The artist is just simply a man who doesn't find life to his liking. He protests. That is all. You would do it one way, I have done it another way. My book is me."   WHOSE BOOK?

From age to age controversies arise and fall and arise again in all the arts. The critics define the thrice defined and invent ever new names for immemorial things. Classic, romantic, impressionistic, expressionistic—these are but a few of the sounding words that have filled and fill the world with clamor. There is much confusion and a good deal of strange pride in this little but lasting world of the articulate and often there is anger and strong animosity over such things as free verse or significant form or the doctrine of art as imitation. Artists and critics, quite like statesmen and economists, will not agree in peace upon a few quite simple elementary things. Man needs food and good-will and a rational freedom; he needs expression; he needs to body forth himself, his contact with the universe, his brief, strange, pitiful experience in the sunlight.   VARIATIONS ON AN OLD THEME

But the arts are inadequate. This is the basic consideration that classicist and romanticist, realist and symbolist alike forget. Schools, techniques, methods are but means toward the end of bringing expression a little nearer to experience, art a little nearer to life. We do not mean toward a cold and stripped objectivity. No such thing exists. Once you saw trees at dusk. It is not the trees that constitute the experience; it is the trees plus the you that saw the trees, the you of that perhaps incomparable hour. What painting shall convey that experience in such a manner that it shall remain incomparable, unique, uniquely precious, yet intelligible to all who are attuned to understand forever? Canvas and colored chemicals and a bit of camel's hair—though they perform wonders how can they reach the pang, the delight, the strangeness of that hour, those trees, that *you?*

Music is the happiest of the arts. Here there is no division between form and substance. Experience is immediately rendered, communication is quite direct and pure. Sounds do not speak in terms made up of alien things, as paint must speak in terms of trees and faces, clay in terms of surfaces and bones. Music alone can abstract experience from its objects and thus achieve, almost without effort, timelessness and beauty. Ultra-modern painters, attempting to do the same, tend to fall into grotesqueness and unintelligibility. They seek to render the experience without its content; they substitute an alien and indefinite content. They want a pure thrill and end in confusion.

Literature, as it is the most inclusive and ambitious of the arts, is also the most heartbreakingly difficult, the most soaring and the most defeated. It seeks to render all of experience, not in its isolated moments but in its totality, its becoming, its intricacy, its intellectual background, its absorbing passions. And words, the medium of this art, are both rigid and brittle, both conventionalized and defaced. The medium itself of this art has no plasticity; it consists of hard, worn, recalcitrant fragments like bits of mosaic used a thousand times. Thus it is not surprising that in literature the effort to make art compete with experience should be most multiform and impassioned or that controversies over mood and method should be in this field most lasting and most acrimonious.

The difficulty, which is a noble one and makes any triumph correspondingly splendid, will remain; the acrimony and absoluteness of the contending factions would disappear with the recognition of simple, fundamental facts. All literature seeks to interpret experience. The naturalist does not render the merely objective nor the symbolist or expressionist the merely subjective. Neither exists in isolation. Human experience arises when subject and object meet. No human experience can exist without both factors. The dewy apples of Vergil are neither the unseen fruit of the tree nor the unseeing eye of the poet. They are the poet plus the fruit. Hence the divisions in art are mere divisions of method seeking the same end, trying to snare the same uncapturable prey. Uncapturable! Love, beauty, delight, despair—these in their own nature are beyond singing, beyond words, beyond symbols. Let each artist work in his own way; each way is as good as any if it brings a little closer and makes a little clearer the beauty of things and the tragic pang of life.

CHAPTER FIVE

MASKS

MONEY is tight. Credit is shaken. It is a bad season. People will not go to the theater. Plays fail. The managers are in the dumps. Actors are walking the streets. Week after week the shoddy trade goods of the favorite hacks are thrown on the stage. The gambling becomes feverish. Quietly, in the midst of the noise and dust, the babble and the tinsel, a tragedy appears. The reviewers call it drab and disagreeable and talk pseudo-learnedly of the Manchester School. Must we do that sort of thing—we, too—a nation of forward lookers, cheerers, dwellers in "great valleys"? The curious thing is that the tragedy does not fail. What if Dryden was right? "The spirit of man," he wrote, "cannot be satisfied but with truth or at least verisimility." What if business is bad? What has that to do with the theater—except that theater where the overfed digest their plethoric dinners? "Two places are open," said the starving Viennese of 1919, "the graveyards and the theaters." The theater is not a game. It is spiritual compulsion. Once it celebrated the gods. Now it broods over the

WORLD, WILL, AND WORD

fate of man. Aristotle and Hebbel knew that; even Bossu and Dryden knew it. When I try to recall it to my friends their total reaction is that I once taught in a college. But I address myself to the American dramatist—that almost hypothetical personage that is yet, so surely, on the point of rising into our vision. Do not let the managers deceive you. Do not let the reviewers deceive you. Nor the babblers in clubs. Seventy per cent of the current hacks' theatrical carpentry does not even make money. The gambling is not even good gambling. Nor be deceived, above all, by the nimble college professors who flutter with the winds of shallow popular fallacies in the hopes that their classes may grow and their articles sell. Address yourself, if need be on bread and water, to the eternal theater—not to the game of Broadway, but to the play of Man.

The thing is so simple. The drama shows man acting or suffering. He acts, he suffers, not in the void, not—in his consciousness, at least—at the tug and pull of blind instincts, but upon some spiritual and moral terms. He calls things evil and good and right and wrong and suffers remorse and shame. He always acts and suffers upon definite assumptions, through and by a definite view of the world. Search deep enough any act or pang and you come upon the sufferer's philosophy of life—his notions of good and evil, of the world and God. An old woman sits in a room sewing her shroud. A bruised, sore woman creeps back into a house because the man who owns it is called her husband. A lad in the streets hears a drum and sees a flag and races towards death and doom. These actions require assumptions into which are packed whole histories, mythologies, philosophies. And the idea of an action is of far more startling import, of far more searing terror, than the individual action itself, and plays in which the ideas of actions are brought before the bar of dramatic justice make the mere rattle of action seem as tame and senseless as the movements of little animals. Do not, then, let the reviewers or managers' agents deceive you with their jargon. "A talky play." These are the plays in which the ideas of actions are exhibited and judged. And by these ideas we live and die.

Once the dramatist was content to show merely and acquiescently the actions of men and the ideas that inspired those actions. Yet never for long. In Euripides the ideas themselves begin to be discussed and judged. But even on the lowest plane—the plane of the mere morality disguised or homily set moving—the dramatist is no theatric hack; even on that plane he is conscious of a fervent identification of his own soul with the ideas upon which his contemporaries act, when they act. The drama is always philosophical. When the dramatist is profoundly at one with the ideas upon which his characters act, the play approaches the religious; when he is at variance with those ideas, it is polemical or prophetic. Do not be deceived by this other fallacy: "So and so's plays are not plays; they are pamphlets." In the deeper creative sense all plays are pamphlets—the "Medea" is a pamphlet on the subjection of woman, and "Tartuffe" on the loathsomeness of hypocrisy, and "Faust" on the spiritual energy that turns apparent evil into good. Shakespeare! Yes, I hear that shout. That divine poet and fashioner of men clung, except for moments, to the mediæval identification of the dramatist with the ideas of the world and the will, of good and evil, upon which his characters act. Some heretic thoughts of his own he had, perhaps some towering disillusion at the core of him. But outwardly he accepts the state and the moral life of his time.

He accepts. Another rejects. Here, at all events, is the ground of the matter. Every dramatist accepts or rejects the ideas upon which his characters act. He shapes the consequences of their actions according to his sense of the quality of the ideas that urge them on. Upon his view of the world, upon his reaction to moral ideas, will depend his choice and conduct of his fable and the end to which he brings the lives of which he treats. It is a better preparation for the career of a dramatist to have watched the actions of a few villagers and to have brooded over those actions at that spiritual core where criticism and creation are one than to have read all the manuals of play-writing and stagecraft in the world and be an expert on lighting and decoration. Shun the theater. It is a place of confusion for the dramatist. Beethoven wrote his symphonies in a little room. They can be played by twenty men or by a hundred, in a barn or a temple. The mechanism of production is not your business; it is your servant. Your business is with man and his world and the ideas that reconcile him to it or drive him to despair.

There is a matter more troubling and intricate. It is the matter of the will. (I am ashamed of setting down these commonplaces. My excuse is that they are not commonplaces among us. What play on Broadway has one seen criticized for its dealing with the will? It is entertaining or not, cheering or depressing, strong—how, gentlemen, how and why? —or feeble; it will run or it won't.) The drama deals with the will. I repudiate the easier, academic agreement with this statement. It goes on the staggering assumption that there is an abstract entity somewhere in the psyche functioning in the void and called the will. Upon that assumption we have the absurd *volteface*, conversion, easy change of aim, motive, character which breeds the happy ending. It is upon that assumption that the wicked Duke in "As You Like It" went into the forest

> Where, meeting with an old religious man,
> After some question with him, was converted
> Both from his enterprise and from the world;
> His crown bequeathing to his banished brother,
> And all their lands restored to them again
> That were with him exiled.

It is lovely as a legend, but monstrous as a representation of human life.

The dramatist not only has his view of the world by which he judges that of his characters, not only his positive or negative or suspended judgment upon the ideas by which they act within and towards the world of their conception; he must have come to some decision upon the very innermost character of human action itself. For how else can he shape his rhythm of moral values; how else determine upon the progress and direction of his fable; how else, indeed, begin to write at all? He has an imaginative vision springing from a tone, a gesture, an expression once observed. A man is overcome by fate. And the man's fate is woven of small, mean, dusty things, or of things gross and impudent and easily discernible by the practical eye. What is this man? A weakling? He is that to the Broadway melodramatist—to the reviewer who condemned Arthur Richman's "Ambush" on the score that the play's protagonist is "weak." But the serious dramatist cannot avoid these fundamental issues by using an unconsidered word. What is the meaning of "weakness" in such a man? It is that all the uncontrollable forces that have made him have left him spiritually defenseless against the evils with which he contends. He is, whatever he can do, always more full of mercy than his adversaries are of shame. His reflectiveness seeks to fathom their shallow clatter. He attributes to them his feelings, his hesitations, his scruples. He is lost. To make him "strong," in that foolish, popular sense, it would be necessary to remount the streams of his personal and ancestral being to their very source and change that source and so change the world, the universe, the planets, and the constellations. Yes, the dramatist, like the novelist, must transcend (the great modern dramatists do transcend) the rubber stamped classification of human qualities and characters that are cut to the pattern of some foolish "ought-ness," which is, in its turn, derived from human experience, misinterpreted under the sway of myth and ritual and the blind primordial terrors and propitiatory practices of our remotest ancestors. Begin to think and at once the gentleman who condemned Richman's protagonist as a "weakling" becomes an unfathomable and almost fantastic character. But who, in these matters, condescends to think?

What is true of "good" characters is no less true of "evil." So good a playwright as Eugene G. O'Neill permits himself the luxury, costly as it is, of sudden external forces that turn "bad" into "better." He has not yet the sovereign vision. Self-discipline is possible by a character whose self is inherently capable of discipline. We do right, in practical life, to insist on the necessity. We may by that insistence, by the direction of intangible forces, breed more people with the capacities that we desire. There may be more men born who desire more strongly the serenity of self-mastery than the riot of self-expansion. But the dramatist has finished creatures. He takes his people as they come, if you please, from God's hand. He cannot tamper with them. They have no more within than they have. To draw that out to the uttermost nerve—such is the fruit of his extremest effort.

It is, then, his vision of the world and of the will that dictates the dramatist's choice and treatment of a fable. Accident has nothing to do with it; ingenuity has nothing to do with it. You hear stories of plays "tinkered with on the road." Mr.

WORLD, WILL, AND WORD

Belasco takes a manuscript and rewrites it. A dramatist whose play can be "tinkered with" or rewritten or revised by an alien hand has not begun to comprehend the elementary conditions of any art. His play may not be inevitable under the aspect of eternity. He is but a man. He is, perhaps, but a manikin. But it must seem inevitable to him. It must be so interwoven with his profoundest perceptions, instincts, convictions, that he is willing to labor for it, starve for it, die for it. Unless it is an inseparable part of his own soul's integrity—it is nothing. Why have the managers the habit of demanding changes, revisions, adaptations for the needs of this season, that theater, a certain star? Because they were not dealing with dramatists at all, but with mechanics, journeymen, hacks. There can be no compromise on this question. This is the final test. Do you think that your play can be changed by another or for another's convenience or use? Destroy it and work with your hands. This does not mean that your play is perfect. Having destroyed it, you yourself may relive its sources in experience, dig deeper into your own soul, and create it afresh. But if Mr. Belasco thinks he can use it, after laying upon it a judicious hand, be sure that only the fire will cleanse it and your shame.

There remains dialogue—the word. I know two hacks who put their ingenuities together and assemble a group of stupid accidents which they call a plot. Then their great effort is over. They run off for a week-end to Atlantic City to write the play. It seems to them a small matter. But consider the word. Into these sound symbols we call speech are packed how many centuries of human experience, how much of universal hope and anguish! All words are flesh. All words are revelation. Try to pluck asunder your highest ecstasy, your most rending grief, your central conviction from the word that expresses it. You cannot. The spiritual universe which man has built is built of things and thoughts crystallized into speech. It is not built of the things and thoughts themselves, but of speech. Whoever writes at all has the double task—to use speech significantly and freshly, to reach through it to the concrete realities which it both reveals and conceals. The dramatist's writing task, which looks so simple, is the most difficult of all. He must use exclusively the speech of others, never of himself. And we must believe that those others are speaking, each in his own tongue, each out of the depth of his own experience, his own unique personality, his own reaction towards world and will and flesh and spirit. Yet from the speech of these others we must overhear—from their speech and not through some cheap device of *raisonneur* mouthpiece—the dramatist's judgment, understanding, compassion, faith. Such is the fundamental creative problem of dramatic dialogue. There are lesser ones. How little speech, in mere quantity, can the dramatist give! Discussions that rise towards a culmination in human fates take weeks, months, years. People eat breakfast in silence. They wrangle on some forenoon. An evening comes on which they fling at each other those impassioned confessions that constitute the drama of life. These millions of words the dramatist must sum up in a few hundred. But the few hundred must have the effect of the millions. We must feel that all necessary speech has been spoken and all the dim places of the soul touched with light. We must feel that each speaker in the drama has stated his case before that eternal judgeless bar—his whole and sufficient case. Good dramatic dialogue is like a blueprint that must yet seem to us to be the finished house; like a thin symbol that must never let us suspect it is not the thing symbolized itself. You will not write good dramatic dialogue on a week-end trip. You must listen to men and women. You must listen with the ear and the heart and the mind. Then, perhaps, in long vigils of a high awareness of mortality it will be given you to write the word that will express your creatures and their struggles with the world and your deep sense of the meaning of those struggles and a dramatic scene will be born.

How well I know the reaction that such considerations get from happy, popular playwrights and smart critics and facile lecturers. Not that way lie the lights of Broadway, they think, or the seven per cent on the second five thousand of weekly box office receipts. Let them not be too sure. But the coming American dramatist with whom I am concerned will not care, will not consciously during the process of creation—however much and rightly he may later enjoy reward—be busy with these matters, but with the world, the will, the word. One danger is his, especially if he is young. And he must be young. Since all his elders and teachers will be married to the trickery, elegantly disguised sometimes, of the theatric trade, he will be ashamed of the apparent priggishness of clothing these easy and worldly matters in what he will be told is mystic cant. Let him remember a great phrase of Molière. "On se rirait de vous," says the pliant Philinte. And Alceste answers: "Tant pis pour qui rirait!"

THE FOREIGN CRITIC: You share my view, then, that the American drama is really entering upon a creative stage?

THE AMERICAN CRITIC: Those words are too big. There is a faint voice; it cries in a howling wilderness.

THE FOREIGN CRITIC: How pessimistic you are!

THE AMERICAN CRITIC: The Pulitzer prize has just been given to "Icebound."

THE FOREIGN CRITIC: And isn't "Icebound" a work of considerable merit?

THE AMERICAN CRITIC: It is a work of some merit. But do you know anything about its author, Mr. Owen Davis?

THE FOREIGN CRITIC: Very little, I confess.

THE AMERICAN CRITIC: Mr. Davis has been writing plays for exactly twenty-five years. He has written one hundred plays. Of these fifty were melodramas produced by Mr. A. H. Woods between 1902 and 1910. Can you quite imagine a prize of the French Academy or the Schiller or Kleist prize going to a gentleman with such a history? Heaven knows I have a small opinion of prizes and prize awards of any sort. But this particular award throws light upon a peculiar American situation.

THE FOREIGN CRITIC: I see perfectly. There is no understanding and respect for the artist or the life of art.

THE AMERICAN CRITIC: No understanding, no deep sense for it. To the committee which made this award it was not at once unimaginable that the author of those fifty melodramas could write a work truly memorable and delicate. Fancy Ibsen, Hauptmann, Galsworthy, even Donnay or Halbe writing fifty melodramas. They could not have done it if the alternative had been literal starvation—not because they like hunger or are conscious of a mission —that, heaven help us, would be the common interpretation—but because their minds would have been nauseated at the very thought.

THE FOREIGN CRITIC: Your point is perfectly clear to me and perfectly elementary. Haven't all your critics made it?

THE AMERICAN CRITIC: No; for to our critics art is neither passion nor vision. They are very able, very honest, very well-informed, and very witty. But, to put it mildly and yet correctly, they don't care enough.

THE FOREIGN CRITIC: I have read some very able reviews.

THE AMERICAN CRITIC: Undoubtedly. But weren't they all—reflect on that a moment—quite worldly?

THE FOREIGN CRITIC: That is not so clear to me.

The American Critic: Do you remember a play called "Roger Bloomer"?

The Foreign Critic: Very vividly.

The American Critic: The play was crude and young and neither thought through nor wrought out. But it was the cry of youth and passion and rebellion—the authentic and everlasting cry of the life of art.

The Foreign Critic: That is why I valued it.

The American Critic: Exactly. And none of the reviewers wrote of this play from within that everlasting life of art of which they should have been a part; they treated it with the superciliousness and faint contempt and smiling incredulity with which the polite world always treats the artist and prophet and outcast and child of light. They said in effect: What shocking manners! What ill-assorted clothes! Pray, dear young man, if you have talent, be proper and show it in a proper way.

The Foreign Critic: You think, then, that your critcism is partly responsible for the slow growth of your dramatic literature?

The American Critic: I do. The young playwright is shy and criticism provides no atmosphere in which he can lose his shyness and speak forth his ardors. Criticism does not sufficiently guard him from the Philistine world; it allies itself with that world.

The Foreign Critic: What an unusual situation. For the past hundred years, at least, it has been both the pride and the chief business of every reputable European critic to be torch-bearer and intermediary, to tilt against the brutishness or indifference of the world, to provide an atmosphere in which genius, which is always strange and new and electrical and estranged, can live and flourish.

THE AMERICAN CRITIC: It is not so among us. A charming and elegant and worldly play—true enough to amuse, not true enough to wound—that is what our critics like. A play like Frederick Lonsdale's "Aren't We All?" at the Gaiety brings out the best that is in them. And the piece is indeed admirable and the acting of both Cyril Maude and Leslie Howard beyond praise.

THE FOREIGN CRITIC: But it is also perfectly barren and perfectly unimportant.

THE AMERICAN CRITIC: Precisely. But our reviewers do not really like the rich, dark, significant folk-play, as they showed in their attitude to "A Square Peg," nor are they, with few exceptions, quite happy or comfortable in the presence of such bitter creative irony as we had in "The Adding Machine."

THE FOREIGN CRITIC: They are in the state in which vital and immediate art troubles them?

THE AMERICAN CRITIC: Yes; and to guard themselves from it they are initially unsympathetic.

THE FOREIGN CRITIC: They, too, want to laugh.

THE AMERICAN CRITIC: I am almost afraid so. Nothing better could happen to the American drama than that some of the chief reviewers should have some shattering experience, like a great and unhappy passion. But they are far too much at ease in Zion to risk it.

THE FOREIGN CRITIC: What a thing to wish your friends!

THE AMERICAN CRITIC: But think how it would improve their work! And work comes first.

THE PROFESSOR: I've been reading Granville Barker's "The Exemplary Theater" with a good deal of satisfaction.

THE DRAMATIC CRITIC: I've read it, too. But I don't think it's important.

THE PROFESSOR: If you'll let me be frank I think I can account for your dislike of it. Barker pleads for the theater as fundamentally an educational force and a form of social service.

THE DRAMATIC CRITIC: Exactly.

THE PROFESSOR: I don't at all blame you for disliking terms besmirched by every Philistine and cheap reformer. But one can carry that dislike so far as to discredit the true and fine and necessary things which those words denote.

THE DRAMATIC CRITIC: I don't discredit those things. But I'm sure the theater is not an educational force and if I'm to call it a form of social service it must be according to an interpretation of my own which will please neither Barker nor yourself.

THE PROFESSOR: Then you are content to have the theater considered an amusement?

THE DRAMATIC CRITIC: As you like.

THE PROFESSOR: You are holding an idea in reserve. You are not, after all, so largely preoccupied with something that is only an amusement.

SPEAKING OF THE THEATER

THE DRAMATIC CRITIC: I dislike these fixed terms. They have a way of betraying you to all sorts of people and committing you to all kinds of causes.

THE PROFESSOR: Very well. But there must be some form, if not formula, by which you can communicate your sense of the value which the theater represents.

THE DRAMATIC CRITIC: It is not so simple. When I was young I was interested in art. Then the theater, except at its rare best, didn't interest me at all. Now I'm interested in life and in art primarily as it interprets and shapes life, and so the theater seems to me very important.

THE PROFESSOR: Why, on account of that shift in your interests, precisely the theater?

THE DRAMATIC CRITIC: There are two reasons. The form of the drama is no accidental one. Its struggle, crisis, resolution are of the essence of the life-process itself. It is thus that life proceeds; it is thus that single lives proceed. Therefore the mirror which the drama holds up to nature gives back an image that is closer to the inevitable laws of being than the image of the other arts.

THE PROFESSOR: But that does not apply to the popular theater.

THE DRAMATIC CRITIC: It applies in a negative sense. The popular playwright must, by an implication that is inescapable in his medium, deal with essentials. He deals with them absurdly. It is easy to shatter his structures. But always the dealing is with essentials. Even assent to the moral order of a silly play is a more tonic exercise for the crowd than mere story interest in cheap fiction. Your very shop-girl, moreover, who does not know what criticism is may look into the reviews of a piece that has moved or amused her and be plunged, upon some terms however crude, into a discussion concerning the world and the will and the true character of human action.

THE PROFESSOR: In brief, the theater's function, in your opinion, is to enlighten people.

THE DRAMATIC CRITIC: That is a terrible word. Yes, I think the theater does throw light. But I am not concerned, like your professional enlighteners, with the light. I am concerned with the thing lit. So far as I can see the worst thing in the world is the avoidable moral suffering. It can be mitigated by understanding man and human life as they really are. All art can serve that purpose; the theater can serve it more directly, swiftly, intensely.

THE PROFESSOR: I am amused to find you so much of a moralist after all.

THE DRAMATIC CRITIC: We are all concerned with conduct. It only depends how or with what intention. I don't want to lay down laws. I want people helped to discover those laws of their own being in the light of which they can live without cruelty or tyranny or rancor.

THE PROFESSOR: I think that I follow you. But did you not have a second reason?

THE DRAMATIC CRITIC: I have already stated it. The drama not only deals with the life-process

SPEAKING OF THE THEATER

upon its own terms, but does so with unexampled intensity. The theater is the instrument by which that intensity is achieved. No artistic experience, that is, no vicarious and interpretative experience of life, can cleave so deep as a theatric one. In those two hours of overwhelmingly profound absorption in something beyond the *ego*, cruelty may melt into compassion, tyranny into tolerance, blindness into vision.

THE PROFESSOR: Does it happen often?

THE DRAMATIC CRITIC: Does anything desirable or of good report happen often? It does happen; it can happen. Yes, I have heard quite simple people discuss plays and admit naïvely that they gained a clearer idea of life from them and were able to act more tolerantly and less muddily and angrily as a result.

THE PROFESSOR: But isn't that both education and social service?

THE DRAMATIC CRITICS: It has, at all events, nothing to do with either information or uplift. For what it comes to ultimately is this: the drama communicates a sense of the necessarily tragic character of human life, of its necessary and inevitable defeat upon any but spiritual terms, of the fact that its single spiritual victory consists in compassion, in understanding, in abstention from force, from moral fraud, from judgment and the execution of judgment.

THE PROFESSOR: In short, you like the theater because, in the long run, you think it will make your views of life prevail?

THE DRAMATIC CRITIC: I do. And I am yet to see a really grown-up person who likes anything very deeply for any other reason.

SPEAKING OF THE THEATER

As Danced by M. Kotchetovsky in the Second Program of Nikita Balieff's Théâtre de la Chauve-Souris

THE CLOWN

I

"LET us dance sadly. All things reel
Slung to the spokes of some vast wheel.
Let us dance sadly. Help is none
For any soul under the sun.

"I am shaken not as I have been shaken
By other woes on other days:
Nothing we hunt is overtaken,
Nothing but dust is on these ways.
Friend sees not friend, lover slays lover,
Self-consumed are delight and desire;
So I dance, having given over
Error and ecstasy, flight and fire.

"So I dance. But not as dances
One who faints to make beauty yield,
I am flung forth as men fling lances
Over a stricken field.

"With stagnant winds I falter,
With crumbling leaves I race,
There is nothing to sting or alter
This foolish face."

II

"You are not to fancy, ladies and gentlemen, that I always wore this red, woolly wig or dipped my face in flour. I was very human once with yellow

THE CLOWN

hair and a physiognomy of my own. A house was mine and patriotic opinions and, though you may not believe it, love. The house became a prison, yet I had nowhere else to go; patriotism became a sentence of death, yet I thought there was still wine left in my goblet; love talked tirelessly of unselfishness and asked my soul to be a slave. I went to wise men and to wise men's books, for I was a modest and tractable fellow. The wise men nodded their heads and spoke many words. And the sum of their wisdom was this: Everything seems to be true and its contrary seems to be equally true, and what right have you—this each wise man added in an angry voice—to doubt that my system rationalizes the universe and dissolves all discords into harmony? . . . At length I fled forth from my house that was a prison, from the state that was a murderer, from love that was a slave-driver. In the autumn field I saw over the stubble a dry blade of wheat dancing in the keen wind under the faint sunlight. It was on that day I bought me this reddish, woolly wig and this absurd bag-like garment and dipped my face in flour and began to dance sadly this dance of sorrowful forgetfulness."

III

"I dance. Ah, yes. But when the last moments come
Something in me breaks through the autumnal hum
Of Chopin's music. Suddenly this is
No more a mimicry of futilities,
But youth, an orchard in bloom, and two soft lips,
A book of verse in the grass, warm finger-tips
Upon my hand, and something in the wind

That could bring balm to hearts unmedicined
Forever by all other healing things.
Or else a night of vision filled with wings
And wonder, when the secrets of sea and land
Pulsed like a living bird within my hand;
Or gentle twilit moments undefiled:
My mother, at her window, with her child. . . .

"That is why, at the end, this poor clown lies
Beyond the curtain with his hidden eyes,
Lest you see tears obliterate the trace
Of cosmic folly from his human face."

CHAPTER SIX
LITERATURE AND LIFE

WHEN his dark hours are upon him the man of letters will often envy the practitioners of other arts. Their medium is so fresh and plastic, his own so stained and rigid. Theirs is free and self-existent, his is entangled in all the base uses of the world. He listens to the third Étude of Chopin, to the Andante of Beethoven's twenty-third sonata, and he despairs. Such divine freedom and purity of utterance is not for him. The dust of all trodden ways blows on his lips; the sound of all harsh and meaningless voices is in his ears. There are glossy shadows on the broad, bright stream; a shiver runs rustling through the innumerable leaves of a tree. So long as he contemplates these objects—identifies himself with them or absorbs them into himself—he is safe. The moment he speaks, his agony begins. For the names he uses are the names neither of these things nor of his vision of them, but of a thousand blunted perceptions and half-obliterated memories. He cannot, like the musician, invent an expression never heard before. He must take the shabby old names of things and, by a

THE PARADOX OF LITERATURE

trickery that threatens always to make an artifice of his art, seek to lend them some freshness and immediacy and sting. And even while he labors thus, he loses bit by bit the uniqueness of his relation to the things contemplated, which alone made his moment worth recording.

He is in far worse case when he comes to deal with the operations of the mind and, above all, when he deals with moral qualities and moral facts. The names by which these go are of a Byzantine conventionalism—remote and bloodless and inflexible. He may mean to bless and succeed in cursing. For his words bristle with alien angers and false judgments and with all the moral rancor of the dead. Let him speak of a noble selfishness, and he will be accused of vain singularity; or of a spiritual use of sensual experience, and he will be held to blaspheme. For these words have so lost touch with the facts of life, and have become so merged in a militant conceptualism, that men no longer use them to name things, but rather do violence to all things in order to crush them into what is considered the appropriate conceptual mold. This they do with the fervor of conviction, and will damn the artist in moral shadings as defending things that rarely exist except in the form of those dour and empty names. But since men are willing to suffer hunger and disease, to fight and to die for these names, it is clear that the artist in literature will often himself be snared by them. So that, in order to speak beautifully and truly, he must struggle not only against the dead weight of nearly all his fellows, but often against the confusions of his own mind. Let him love liberty and praise it, some one will discover that he has counseled license. The ugly word may startle him and even keep him from seeing that no such thing exists, but that it is a name men use for stigmatizing the liberties which they themselves do not want to exercise.

It is, when one reflects, as though from the beginning man had been haunted by a great fear, and in that fear had sought deliberately to darken and to simplify the beautiful and various world as well as his own subtle and divided heart. Thus he took all sharp perceptions and unborrowed passions and far-ranging thoughts, and gave to these infinitely multiform things a few quite bleak and rigid names. And the power of these names in keeping out freedom and fear was such that he came to believe that they exhausted the varieties of his experience, and grew angry if anyone offered to extend his narrow world a little farther toward the wide boundaries of reality. The proof of this unconscious process is marvelously revealed when one compares different languages and the people who speak them. There are languages that contain names for moods and for moral perceptions and distinctions, as well as for qualities in the external world, that are blankly absent from our own. Are we then incapable of these moods and perceptions? No; for we acquire them when we perfectly acquire that other tongue. But so long as we are confined to one language we are imprisoned within the moral twists and self-imposed limitations of those dead speakers of it who checked the growth of certain moods and perceptions and distinctions by giving them either deprecating names or the names of other things. Thus men have named things out of existence, and actually impoverished human life by forcing upon delicate and subtle phenomena, both of the world and of the mind, the harsh names of what all knew and approved. This universal nominalism is far more dangerous than is commonly thought; it can drain life and kill things and cripple the soul.

This, then, is the paradox of literature. The artist desires to reveal and interpret reality. But he must use a medium built from the beginning to darken and conceal it. Not until he is himself liberated from the medium of his art can he begin to practice it truly; not until he has died to all words can the world be born again in his own soul. He must return to the eternally concrete and name no thing until he has grasped it in its real nature, nor compare it to another until he has known it to be essentially incomparable. To know human thoughts and actions he must have learned to see them as unique and without name; he must recover a complete innocence of vision and let no words betray him into violating it. And when he has done all that and has at last made himself worthy of his art—then comes his hardest hour. He cannot, after all, invent new symbols; he is bound to the use of speech. Now that he knows the full treachery of words, he must use them to reveal that very treachery and to lead men back to all the things these words have stunted or defamed or left unspoken. He has substituted realities for myths in his own mind, but myths are all he has with which to body forth realities in art. He shifts the meaning of a symbol here and alters a connotation there. For all that, he has the fore-knowledge of ultimate failure. All that he says will still hide his direct vision of reality and leave his agonies and exaltations blurred and dim.

THE PARADOX OF LITERATURE

Yet his career of failure is not without its luminous moments. His aim is so high that a fleeting success reconciles him to his fate. For such success is, in the truest sense, creative. It gives men not only beauty but vision, not only delight but life. It increases the number of living realities, extends the possibilities of experience, and creates both things and thoughts that would else be lost to the consciousness of man. This is what the ten thousand scribblers do not understand. They heap words upon words and tribal formularies on tribal formularies. They circulate an obliterated coinage; they shuffle brass instead of minting gold. The true artist in letters gives life and creates freedom. In the paradox of literature he finds both his pain and his reward. His success is difficult and rare. But when it comes, it breaks the fetters of the world and adds to the sum of our unalterable good.

Poets are fond of talking about music. What they commonly mean is the cadences of verse or the music of the spheres. Concerning the art in its stricter sense they know little or nothing. It is true that Campion was an exquisite composer and that Milton played the organ. But music in the six-

THE TWO HARMONIES

teenth and seventeenth centuries was a simple thing. What the poet then meant by music was a grave and lovely air. Whoever has heard the old music played on flutes and virginals and recorders knows that a difference in degree has almost become a difference in kind between it and the "Feuerzauber" or Debussy's "Gardens in the Rain."

In later ages the alienation of literature from music, especially in the English-speaking countries, became more and more complete. Browning was an exception; so, in a different way, was Sidney Lanier; so, in still another manner, is Arthur Symons. Far more representative was Tennyson, who had, notoriously, as little ear as Charles Lamb himself. From the works of most of the major poets and prose writers you would hardly suspect the immense influence and importance of music in the modern world. Hazlitt and even Shelley wrote about painting. Neither in their works nor in the works of the men that followed them will you find so much as the name of a great composer. With the rise of the novel, those in which music figures largely were bound to make a sporadic appearance. But most of them, like the once well-known "The First Violin," by Jessie Fothergill, are shoddy and sweetish, and George Moore's "Evelyn Innes" still remains a glorious exception to an all but universal rule.

Nor, in view of present developments, is the breach between the two great sister arts likely to disappear. Many lettered people love music. But they want it to be pure music. They turn to it precisely because it liberates them from the inveterate intellectualism, the strain and debatableness of words. There is no argument in a gavotte by Händel or a waltz by Brahms; nothing needs refutation in the Larghetto of Tchaikowsky's Fifth Symphony; the riddle of the painful earth—which is, somehow, inherent in every word one utters—does not leap at you from either the Adagio of Beethoven's Sonata Pathétique or from the Andante of his Twenty-third. Here is pure beauty of form, pure wholeness of feeling. Into this art one can cast one's entire soul, lose one's entire self, and in that loss know peace. Wagner, too, is a great favorite of lettered hearts. He is almost as mighty a melodist as Beethoven himself and where he insists on meaning something beyond the reach of pure music he has, himself a poet, a dramatist, and even a critic, provided a literary substructure that is native to the writer's and the thinker's bent of mind.

It is when music begins to poach on his preserves that the literary artist loses patience. Not out of envy, heaven knows. But if it will not sing him out of himself and into ecstasy, its uses to him are gone. He can *say* things so much more adequately and subtly and profoundly himself. He resents the orchestral intricacies that overlay the melodic groundwork even in Richard Strauss's "Don Juan." He wants thematic material that is musically well defined, that is beautiful, that makes him feel. Tonal arabesques tease him; tonal description and cerebration make him smile. No, it is not necessarily ignorance. He is often quite aware of what the composer is driving at and can even recognize it

<small>THE TWO HAR-
MONIES</small>
when some ultra-modern plays with unrelated keys. But he knows how heartbreakingly difficult it is to say things in words, which are the natural instruments of speech. He knows that all songs must, from the nature of things, be songs without words. He wants to be spared the stammering and stuttering of a medium which, in its proper use, he often thinks more beautiful and certainly diviner than his own.

<small>DATED AND
DATELESS</small>
In recent literary conversation one is constantly hearing the word "dated." It is used superciliously; it is used with an air of finality. It is designed to convey the fact that the piece of writing thus characterized is so implicated with the special and narrow problems of its moment in history as to have lost all meaning and marrow, all validity and worth. We have heard "Mme. Bovary" called "dated" and dismissed, and Shaw's "Candida" and Sudermann's "Magda" and Hauptmann's "Lonely Lives"; we have heard the frothy and over-eager fling their "terribly" or "quite frightfully dated" at Gissing and the Goncourts, at the later works of Hervieu and the earlier ones of Wagner, and we have often wondered whether, upon this view, everything in literature is not "dated" unless its date is today.

This is a curious way of judging books, and points to an equally curious idea of the nature of art. It takes the uncommon, and fancies it to be the rule. A work profoundly and passionately implicated with the problems of its own period is implicated with the problems of all. For only the outer aspect of the problem changes; its essence is as enduring as that human nature from which it has sprung. The really "dated" artist is he who never wrestled with a problem nor went to the root of any matter. Such a one is rarely remembered long enough to be called anything by an impatient posterity. There is, to illustrate from another art, Bouguereau. He is indeed incredibly "dated." You look at those expanses of perfect skin in his canvases and wonder. The heads give him away. Those praying or singing females have no relation to reality and its ways at all. They embody a simper that was once thought merely proper and a sentimentality that was always repudiated in the inwardness of the earnest mind. "Dated" art deals with no problem, is sunk in no foundation, is not concrete, and therefore not universal. Given the right depth and nobility of execution all problems are today's as well as yesterday's, and the war against which Aristophanes protested is as richly woven into man's lasting fate as that which today threatens the same shores and capes.

We suspect, however, that the recent prevalence of this particular way of regarding books and plays has nothing to do with any reflection on the nature of the artistic process. It seems rather to spring from something akin to what the psychoanalysts call a defense complex—an instinctive deprecation of what is too severe, arduous, troubling. If "Candida" were "dated" and done with, for instance, the problem of that woman's relations to the two men in the play would be solved and transcended and life, by

DATED AND DATELESS so much, easier and simpler. Nothing, of course, could be further from the truth. Most people are not yet clear enough on the nature of the case to state it to themselves; they muddle along as helplessly as ever, and Shaw's creative instruction may be received by the twenty-first century. If Hauptmann's "Rose Bernd" is "dated," we may be comforted by the thought that her story and her fate could happen no more. Alas, it happened yesterday in the Spoon River and will happen tomorrow in Winesburg, and if in these places and in Gopher Prairie its action is more hushed and more swiftly covered by the waters of convention and seemliness, that difference is a superficial and transitory one. The tragic facts remain, the human cry of passion and confusion, the accusation and the piteous end. Rose Bernd is in our villages and Emma Bovary parades on Fifth Avenue every pleasant afternoon. It matters little that once she wore a chignon and now bobs her hair. Jack Tanner flees from Anne along every highway and the Johannes Vockerat of "Lonely Lives" is to be found on every college campus in America. All art is dated in the sense that it uses the changing externals of the human show; all profoundly sincere art is dateless in the precise measure in which it deals with concrete problems of fate and character and circumstance. In these is the eternal, constant, enduring, which is nothing less than the nature of mankind itself. Abstraction and falseness only are ephemeral. That which has once flung roots deep into the mother earth remains.

Good plays and novels and stories of real experiences that are told one by serious people all center about some conflict among men and women. And the more deeply one searches the clearer grows the fact that all the persons engaged in this conflict are good. None of them are conscious of evil or of a desire for evil. When disaster comes they are all equally astonished and equally sorrowful. Some of them will become self-righteous and thus build a defensive armor about the inner ache. But that is as near villainy as one gets. Consider, from this point of view, the better fiction of the day and hour. There are no villains in it. There are helpless people, perverse people, angry and confused people. There is no Mr. Hyde; not even an Iago. The conflicts, whether in life itself or transferred from life to literature, are none the less harsh and bitter. Men fight and wound and wound themselves for philosophies invented five thousand years ago. They suffer for immemorial fetishes; their hearts bleed for taboos as old as Tut-Ankh-Amen's tomb.

Of all the notions that create conflict the most persistent and deadly is that which regards the world of nature and of moral experience as fixed and finished. From it arise all the forces of repression and false authority. The tyranny of parents and teachers which is often so pathetically well meant, the fierce torments endured and inflicted by jealous people, both arise from this frantic clutch of the mind on the notion that things must not change, shall not change, that life and nature are frozen into patterns that endure. It is not surpris-

CONFLICT

ing that it should be so. In the total life of man the heliocentric theory is of yesterday, the theory of evolution almost of today. What power has the average man's superficial assent to these cold and alien theories against the fierce emotional certainties distilled into his very blood from a thousand ancestors? His mind may have its moments of clarity. At the urgency of any passion—love, fear, jealousy, patriotism—these foreign laws of some scientist's making are swept away. Our man at once becomes at one with his remotest ancestors and fights without relenting for a world in which children must obey, love must not change, impossible pledges must be self-perpetuating, and his country, right or wrong, must be victorious upon bloody fields.

When we leave the average and enter the society of thoughtful and instructed people we still find that perpetual conflict. Here there is often vision; rarely is there any power. Men and women who, in their intellectual tasks, assume instinctively the dynamic character of the universe, of life and experience as synonymous with growth, change, decay, will, in any matter that affects the personal life, cling emotionally to that ancestral picture of a static world. Cultivated women will insist that emotional change is crime; enlightened parents will attempt to bend the unbendable will of the generation to come; statesmen will insist that to question the acts of their forerunners is treason. In brief, our emotions embrace one theory and one vision of things, our minds another. Action lags a thousand years behind thought; we are civilized only from the neck up. We use science for destruction, not for liberation; we know that the lightning is not the thunderbolt of Zeus, but our emotional reactions and actions in the conduct of life are generally those of the trembling barbarian who sacrifices a sheep to avert the anger of his god. What is needed to make life more peaceful and more honorable is a re-education of emotions, an effort to bring the emotional life in harmony with the life of the mind. Conflict will soften and moral suffering will grow less acute as our hearts and minds draw nearer to each other across the gulf of the ages. Our great hope is that they may some day be contemporaries. _{CONFLICT}

The long-haired poet is an anachronism; the man of letters scorched by the fires of life and art is almost as extinct as the tavern in which he once held forth. Our Latin Quarter is a place of feeble gestures and of furtive hunger for the fleshpots of success. What would we make of a Sainte-Beuve, either the man or the critic? Our poets and novelists and playwrights own motor cars and country houses; they play golf and discuss the coming election. On some of them the varnish of the sound and reliable citizen shows cracks. But they are all busy covering the flaws. Their walk and conversation are one long act of deference to the standards of real estate and wholesale poultry. Though dedicated to so uncommon an activity, they nurse a frantic fear of the abnormal and are the first people in recorded

SYSTEM AND STRAWBERRY-CRUSH

SYSTEM AND STRAWBERRY-CRUSH

history to attempt the production of literature which they have not first lived.

Youth seems to offer exceptions. But the first thousand dollar check is the beginning of the end. To earn others you must not offend the heavy advertisers who indirectly but implacably control the editorial policy of the great magazines by which such checks are issued. Thus by a process at once brutal and insidious the gentlemen who pay fabulous advertising rates in order to commemorate on gorgeous pages such legends as "Keep your car young!" or "Drink Strawberry-Crush!" contribute their mite toward keeping our literature sane and safe. The recipient of their indirect bounty who once, perhaps, by the lakes of Wisconsin or the yellow waters of the Congaree saw the eternal fevered vision of art, hires a secretary and moves uptown. A house in the country will come later. One can't bring up children in the city. Our man of letters starts a serial. He fortifies himself with strawberry-crush.

A commoner situation is different and more magnificent. Lion and lamb gambol together on the tennis courts. No longer does an irate father—white whiskers, face a bit ruddy from port—disown his wild-eyed offspring who would be a poet. The father has shed whiskers and port and is at peace with his son. If the boy wants to go in for the drama, he proceeds to Harvard; if for the short-story, there is Columbia. The early years may be lean. But so they are in other professions. It is a pity the boy will not go into business. Well, this is a world of trials. And there is, the son assures him, a business side to writing. There are actual trade journals. Take the one that discovered and practically made Jack London. Everybody knows what his income was! In the February number, for instance, there's a corking article by L. Harcourt Farmer called "The Business of Writing." "Listen to this, Dad: 'We know that the men and women who are out to do big stuff, to make a living, have system for their middle name!'" Two fingers of the father's efficient hand go up to his youthful, close-clipped mustache. He looks out over the trim lawn. "But how about those parlor Bolshevist writers in New York that you hear about nowadays?" "Aw, they're not in it!" The son is cheery and full of rich assurance. "You never see their names in ———." And he mentions the periodicals to which he aspires. He studies the type of story which each of them affects—big business, heart interest, adventure. He notes plot variations and the niceties of effective structure. He records the results of his observations in a card catalogue. System is his middle name.

Old discords are silenced. There is peace where there should be a sword. It has come because we are so desperately afraid of losing our lives in order to gain them. Doubtless the history of literature is a sorry one on its economic and, if you will, its moral side. Who would see his son risk the fate of Otway in the London alleys, of Verlaine in jail or hospital? Not the snug citizen of any age. He has never, to be sure, been as careful of life in mines

SYSTEM AND STRAWBERRY-CRUSH

or wars. But that is an old failing of his. It is the son who, today and here, threatens to play us false. It is he who has dared hunger and disease and scorn for the creative vision. If he turns timid and does not hold the world well lost, we had better stop prating about literature.

In the Old South committees of gentlemen used to meet from time to time and finance mighty quarterlies and pass resolutions establishing a Southern literature. We smile at them. But our courses of instruction in creative letters and our trade journals are quite as futile and a bit more vulgar. For the artist, good fellow-citizens, is what he is neither through affectation nor viciousness. Resolutions and courses of instruction will palm off on you but a dreary substitute. Unless he hurts you, he is an impostor. When he crashes through your favorite delusions and deals freely with the stuff of life you fancy fixed and rigid, then you may know he is with you—enemy and outcast of your today, friend and guide of all your tomorrows. Somehow he will conquer for himself both suffering and wine. He cannot live on system and strawberry-crush.

THE MARKETPLACE

The arts, no less than trade, have their marketplace. It is a gay scene and an attractive one. There are endless parties at luncheon and dinner and at midnight; there are premières at playhouses; there are meetings in publishers' and producing managers' offices. There is next to no ugly chaffering; there is very little niggardliness. A looker-on would say: What good fellows! How much more vigorously art should flourish here than in some shabby Latin Quarter! Everybody is everybody's friend; there is almost no trace of envy or malice. The situation is ideal; it is healthy; it is American.

All that is true. And indeed there is a psychical cleanliness in our better literary life—a genuine comradeliness and decency of contact and attitude —which cannot be too warmly praised. Yet this pleasant market-place of the arts has the dangers of all market-places of any kind in the world, and many a talent has grown thin and withered or smart and brassy here that might elsewhere have acquired richness and color, depth and glow.

The market-place offers substitute satisfactions, *Ersatz*-glory. John Smith has written a good book and some stunning stories. His publishers are satisfied with his sales; the critics, having discovered him, are genially inclined. Maybe there's a play in him. So the folk of the theater are cordial. Smith finds life exhilarating. Perhaps he has behind him years in Grub Street or in some equally disconsolate locality. Is it surprising that his heart feels warmed and his senses eager, that he floats from party to party and feels that life is indeed worth living when, at some distinguished première, he finds that he is surrounded by friends—*in* with the group that "makes" a work of art in America? He throws out his chest; he glows; the years during which he was "out" recede into a dismal and almost unimaginable distance. Failure? He begins to despise it. Look at himself. Why can't everybody do likewise? That eternally protesting, unsuccessful poet of whom he heard yesterday, always disgruntled, always shabby—there must be something wrong with the fellow. There must be. Merit *is* rewarded; the dourest critics unbend to genuine talent. Smith determines that his second book shall be in the vein of his first. He determines this very quietly, in the secret hiding-places of his mind. But the determination is very firm. He cannot bear to lose what he has gained; he must keep his stall in the pleasant sunlight of the market-place.

Thus, it is easy to see, jollity has begotten a dangerous complacency, friendliness has really begotten fear, the outer show of success an inner failure. Smith has lost the remoteness, the necessary solitariness, the self-determination of his creative life. Possessing advantages that he fears to lose and friends whom he must not estrange, having adopted a mode of life which costs so and so much to keep up, he has in reality bartered away his own development as an artist and as a man.

No, we do not mean that the artist must be dour and grim and always out of the pleasant warmth of fellowship—a grumbler and a bear. Let him by all means visit the market-place and, from time to time, share in its jollity and brightness. But let him never be of it, never dependent on it, never a part of it. Somewhere within him, as well as somewhere on the visible earth, there must be a place where his traffic with the "dæmonic" forces is undisturbed. The "dæmon" of Socrates and Goethe must rule with a sway that nothing can essentially impair. There must be no danger of any substitution for the ultimate test of veracity to the inner vision. "Do make your hero a bit more attractive," pleads the most generous of publishers and the best of friends. "It's the women who read the novels. You will be the first to grumble if your royalties drop. Your artistic integrity will not be impaired by making the fellow more likable!" How tempting it sounds and, on a certain plane, how true! And what will be the difference a hundred years hence anyhow? But it is not on such terms that art comes into being. Flee while yet you can! Sunlight steals even into a garret; it floods the hillsides. The market-place is not the only bright place in the world. There are austerer comforts, which are independent of circumstances. These remain.

THE MARKET-PLACE

The advice of Hazlitt to reread an old book whenever one is tempted to read a new one is good advice. But like even the best advice it should be acted on not only not too literally but with moderation. The reading of many years leaves many memories—beautiful and somber, gay and moving. In hours of reverie these memories are part of the mind's best possessions. For reading is deeply rooted in life. It marks high moments, profound consolations, periods of splendor and decline. To have read George Moore's "Confessions of a Young Man" at twenty is something more than reading. It is akin to religion and to love. But shall we reread that book? Heaven forbid! For we can well imagine how cold those palpitating pages would seem today, how drained of what we once brought

ON REREADING

to them, how much of their wisdom would seem knowingness, how much of their beauty to be touched by decay. Not to reread the book—that is the only way of possessing it forever and of possessing untarnished that hour of youth when first it swam into our ken.

This, then, is the true philosophy of the matter. All but the authentic classics, new or old, had better be left alone if we would keep the gifts that they once had to give us. Various temperaments will react toward past reading in various ways. The principle remains. In an idle hour, not long ago, we took up "Lavengro." Once we had almost belonged to what Andrew Lang called the true Borrovians. Alas, we found Borrow amazingly dull, pompous, and wooden. What had once seemed rude manliness now seemed mere ignorant pig-headedness. Did ever mortal know so much with so little result? The experience was a little disconcerting. We had planned to reread some of Dickens, not a little Stevenson, even Trollope. We shall not do so. We shall leave Mr. Micawber alive forever in the chambers of the mind; we shall keep untouched by the morose criticism of the later years the inimitable Alan Breck Stuart; we shall not lose our cathedral closes and towers of Barchester by rashly opening the books that gave them to us once. On a lower plane the counsel to reread is imperative. Long ago we had hours of keen absorption in Walter Besant and in Wilkie Collins; not only in "All Sorts and Conditions of Men" but even in "The Woman in White." We must flee from such books or they are ruined forever. We once tried, for ten horrible minutes, to reread "The History of David Grieve."

The minor Elizabethans share this fate with the minor Victorians. It is no empty observation to make that all the unromantic part of the eighteenth century stands the test of rereading magnificently. As experience and reason ripen one is drawn more and more to the sovereign sanity and simplicity of the books of that age. If Stevenson seems a little thin and tormented, read Defoe's "Captain Singleton;" if all the words of the moderns seem either over-used or over-luscious, read Swift; if poetry seems, in certain moods, to have lost both the ground under its feet and the rhythm of its eternal tread, it is no bad plan to reread the "Epistle to Dr. Arbuthnot" or certain incomparable lines in the "Epistle to Jervas." Addison, to be sure, seems ever more anemic and meanly proper as the years go on. It is a superstition, however, that Johnson is important only as the sitter for a memorable portrait. With all its faults and prejudiced judgments and failures of vision, the "Lives of the Poets" remains one of the sanest, most fascinating, most human books in the language. Nor is this all. It was in the despised *Rambler* that Johnson said he "would not willingly interrupt the dream of harmless stupidity or destroy the jest which makes its author laugh;" it was there, too, that he declared: "It ought to be the first endeavor of a writer to distinguish nature from custom; or that which is established because it is right, from that which is right only because it is established; that

ON REREADING

he may neither violate essential principles by a desire of novelty, nor debar himself from the attainment of beauties within his view by a needless fear of breaking rules which no literary dictator had authority to enact." We may be very mordant wits and very philosophical critics today. We shall not easily beat that.

Yes, the books that bear rereading are the books that have essential sanity and freedom. They may be as lofty as "Faust," or as kneaded of the common clay as the tales of Smollett. It is the overbright that fades, the strained that snaps. An unnatural polish will soon tarnish, and intricate forms not stuffed with substance will crumple, wither, and decay. Johnson's prose is fresher today than Oscar Wilde's, Pope's verses than those of Arthur O'Shaughnessy. Here is a counsel for writers as well as readers. The books that can be reread are the books that are models. The others partake of the nature of dreams, pleasurable but transitory.

JOURNEYING

To stay at home is to embrace too low a view of human nature and too dispiriting a one of the flatness of life. Adventure is to be found, as in other and more brilliant periods, along the road. We live in tight circles, in unescapable coteries. In these groups each is bound to the other by strong though invisible threads of interest, considerateness, prudence. The girl whose father you are bound to meet at luncheon day after tomorrow will not be caught in anything but conventional verbiage with you today; you will discover your best friends on the edge of a reserve that is near neighbor to unveracity because they fear your contacts with still other friends who are not wholly theirs. Or what they say may float, without any fault of yours, to their banker or boss or landlord or father or wife. Thus people who may be truly fond of each other are often to be found in flight from any genuine communion with each other and are struck dumb by the social fears amid which we live.

There are other reasons for the dullness of home. To see people too constantly is not to see them at all. Custom stales one's perceptiveness. Since you have often seen Smith in a dour mood you are blind to the moment when his dourness has a tragic edge. Since Jones is a blithe fellow you take his blitheness for granted; you either do not see the shadow that has crept over it or set that shadow down to indigestion. Smith and Jones are like your boots and your barber. They are familiar and so you expect them to stay common. Anyhow, you have no time. There are letters to be dictated. Let them take their interests and troubles elsewhere.

On a journey you are set free. You use the eyes of the body and the more seeing eyes of the soul. Those who go sight-seeing among buildings and paintings and mountains have, no doubt, an amusing time. To go sight-seeing among people is a more arduous but also a more enduring pleasure. It is, at least, a magnificent temptation and its rewards are great. You come a stranger and are therefore accepted as a friend. You will not stay and gossip; you can betray no one; you are safe. What happens is that the long-curbed passion for communication, for self-communication, breaks forth in your presence. Bring but an understanding look, an interpretative word—a thousand strange and beautiful and significant secrets are your own. They are not always told you in speech. A woman's gesture will beg you to assume her whole heart's history; fat men in smoking-rooms will suddenly reveal strange sparks of poetry at the core of the grimy layers with which they wrap their souls. Often you need but be still with a certain gentle and vigilant stillness to learn more in a week of journeying than in a year at home.

What you learn is wonderfully heartening even though the substance of it is often sad enough. In that icy isolation that is so common among familiars you had almost, perhaps, come to regard yourself as a little monstrous. Others seemed to have sources of life which you could not tap, and thus to possess a content of which you are not capable. You forgot that they, like yourself, carry about on the daily business of life a carefully arranged aspect with which to cheer their families, please their employers, soothe their colleagues. On a journey your own mask drops, and that is the signal for others to ease themselves of theirs. The result is that the flat world takes on brilliancy and splendor; it is seen visibly to shed its dust; it becomes peopled with magnificent persons; it streams with tragic pageantry. You feel suddenly and overwhelmingly at home. The charming woman who saves you, by the gentlest of maneuvers, from a dull and inarticulate party does so in order to tell you a history that is almost visionary in its strangeness and tragic glow; a quiet man on a walk turns out to be a philosopher and a student of human life. At table you heard the woman say sprightly and conventional nothings to her habitual friends and the man preserve a silence to which his familiars were evidently accustomed. But you, who are a stranger, are privileged. You bring with you liberty and speech. Thus you, in your turn, are richly and constantly companioned and find abroad a homelikeness in the world that you had long sought for and sought in vain.

One often hears people object to what they call novels and plays with a purpose; fine works have been condemned for being "mere propaganda;" even distinguished critics join in this thoughtless game. What all these objectors really mean is one of two things: they either do not like the particular brand of propaganda offered them or else they do not like the technical method of its presentation. Propaganda for the known, the accepted, the conventional is not called propaganda. Propaganda for the ordinary pseudo-romantic view of life is called by politer names. When the hundred-per-cent hero wipes the dust with the exotic heretic and the people in the audience applaud in a feeling of self-identification with the hero, they do not know that they are acclaiming propaganda for the things which, according to them, ought to be disseminated and spread abroad.

Such, as every schoolboy ought to know, is the

harmless meaning of that sinister word—things that ought to be made known. Since everyone thinks that there are such things, it follows that all speech, all writing, all art is propaganda. There can be no difference of opinion here. The amusing race of mortals, however, is so made that each calls his own kind of propaganda by a more arrogant and astonishing name, the name of truth. It comes, then, to a question of personality and its tastes in philosophy, morals, politics. "Hic spinas colligit," said the Roman wit, "ille rosas." But since the gatherer of thorns is convinced that they are roses, he cannot be blamed for thinking himself a spreader of truth and him who gathers the flowers a vicious propagandist.

But there is another, perhaps narrower and yet deeper sense in which all great and grave literature is indeed passionate propaganda. Such literature always involves a view of the world, of God, of men's relations to the world and to each other and to God, which is at the very core of the being who is a poet. Not only the bibles of the world—the whole of the Attic drama, the whole of mediæval literature have as their central and controlling motive to justify the ways of God to man. In Shakespeare the theological and metaphysical background is blurred, and propaganda for a moral order, for moral harmony, takes its place; with Molière and Swift we enter the realm of protest and inquiry, of propaganda for reason and freedom, which finds its culmination in Goethe. There is no work of serious literature which does not at its center proceed from a spiritual passion that desires to conquer the world for its objects. The impersonal Flaubert castigated the false romanticism of his characters in the service of clearness and cleanliness; all satire is propaganda for neglected truth, all irony for men's folly in not embracing it. The lyrical cry of Shelley is a cry over the discrepancy between the world of reality and the nobler world of his vision; one poet denies God in order to help man, another cultivates pure beauty as an escape from the inextricable confusion of things, still another as a means toward salvation in itself. But all literature, all art is in its final and ultimate depth an answer to the question: What shall we do to be saved?

The distinction to be made is a distinction of technique. In imperfect works the inevitable propaganda for some truth, some view of life, some road to salvation—whether the propaganda be positive or negative—is not a part of the creative act. It is not organic; it has been fastened on. It is then that we get mere preachment and pamphleteering, whether in the study or on the stage; it is then that the reproach of "mere propaganda" can properly be raised. It cannot be raised because a work of art is rooted in metaphysics. All works of art are. Nor can it be raised because the metaphysics of a particular work of art do not harmonize with our own. All poems, novels, plays are inherently philosophies, cosmogonies, moral universes. All have a purpose. The distinction is not between art that is purposeful or purposeless but between good art and bad.

AN EVER-CHANGING MORAL WORLD

The publication of Sherwood Anderson's "Many Marriages" and the performance of Sholom Asch's "The God of Vengeance" have once more raised through public action and private discussion the question of the relation of literature to morals. We are concerned for the moment with neither the one work nor with the other. We are concerned with the problem of bringing some clarity into the discussion itself, some order into the appalling muddleheadedness from which it seems to proceed.

We wish first to pay our respects to the absolutist point of view. The classical example of that is, of course, the Catholic. If you believe, as you have a perfect right to do, that the rules of human conduct have been eternally fixed by divine revelation, you have logically a perfect right to forbid or to destroy books that by precept or example controvert the divine truth and corrupt the feeble heart. The Index and the inquisition are your proper weapons. Cultivated and humane Catholics do not, as a matter of fact, draw these extreme conclusions. Our point is that their logical position would be unassailable were they to do so.

Our criticism is directed against the men and women who do not profess the absolutist point of view and who nevertheless clamor against works of art that offend their moral tastes or moral sensibilities. And it is a curious observation that many of these men and women are descendants of the Puritans, who were ardent individualists at least in theory and ardent cultivators of the inner light. There is no real breach between the old and great

Protestant doctrine of the individual soul's immediate responsibility to its God, and the words of Emerson, arch Puritan and Protestant himself: "Good and bad are but names, very readily transferable to that or this; the only right is what is after my constitution, the only wrong what is against it."

<small>AN EVER-CHANGING MORAL WORLD</small>

The history of human conduct bears out Emerson's saying in a very practical and objective way, so that it was long ago remarked by Locke that "there is scarce a principle of morality to be named, or rule of virtue to be thought of, which is not somewhere or other slighted and condemned." The moral world, in brief, is a dynamic, a changing world in which change, as in the universe itself, is the condition of progress. Not every proclaimer of change is perfect. But the process itself functions through individuals—artists, thinkers, creative *livers*. We must give these scope to avoid an Egyptian fate. They are few enough. They will often offend our moral sensibilities, since these sensibilities are based on habit which is both easy and dear. There is no other way out. The risk must be taken if there is to be a progressive unfolding of either truth or beauty.

We shall be told that this doctrine of moral relativity sounds well enough but that it leaves us without a criterion, without any practical *modus operandi* in a world that contains—well, *La Vie Parisienne*. But that is an error. In the first place, we have heard of no one objecting to the public sale of *La Vie Parisienne*. It can be had anywhere for the asking. Secondly, no one will accuse that periodical of creative change in the moral world. It is as absolutist as Mr. Sumner. It simply thinks vice more amusing and more profitable than virtue. It is conventional and conformist to the bone. So is all pornography. It counts on the sense of absolute sin, on the conception of human passion as foul and unlawful, on furtiveness, lingerie, and stealth.

AN EVER-CHANGING MORAL WORLD

The good man, said Nietzsche, seeks to preserve that which is, the noble man to create new values. So it is with artists and with books. He is the most moral artist who is most earnestly concerned with the problems of human conduct and is concerned with them creatively. To have a new vision of righteousness, to point a new path to salvation is to share, in however humble and imperfect a manner, the glory of the prophets. To see human life in a fresh and creative way—that is moral even in the most conventional sense. To approve Zane Grey and condemn Sherwood Anderson, whether you agree with him and his methods or not, is a violently immoral proceeding. It is the old, unlearned lesson of "Faust." Perfection is far off. We do not know what it is. To our vision it seems, moreover, dangerously like stagnation, like death. What remains? Experiment, striving through greater error to less, through lower beauty and truth to higher. He who strives thus has done the utmost that is given man to do; him the eternal armies will gladly receive.

THE UNHAPPY GOOD

In a hundred years it will be as though these things had not happened. The human spirit has, after all, a way of marching on. "Clean Book" leagues will

182

not stop the development of literature; fines and imprisonments will not stop dramatists from depicting human life as the spirit that is forever free moves them to depict it, nor will men and women be kept from seeing the plays that please or exalt them. The theory of evolution has really nothing to fear from Mr. Bryan and the noise and anger of the fundamentalists will soon "be with yesterday's sev'n thousand years." Truth ultimately wins its way; you cannot beat beauty in the end. "Securus judicat orbis terrarum."

There is a meantime—a long meantime. And during that period we may wonder at the strange ways of people. There is a little gospel mission around the corner. In front of it, before service time, stands the leader in the coolness of the dusk. He has a New Testament in his hand and his finger is in the book, marking, for all we know, the Beatitudes. You look at him. It is not a happy face that you see; it has no peace in it. It is a belligerent yet defeated face, a repressed and half-angry face, a determined face, almost an embittered one. The man is so busy being right that he never thinks of being happy, so busy being moral that he quite forgets the duty to be good. If we did not fear the imputation of discourtesy we could mention the names of many mighty crusaders in all the causes of "thou shalt not do what I cannot or dare not do," and show the likeness of those faces and the spirits behind those faces to the face and spirit of the leader of the mission around the corner.

There was Miss Ford, the daughter of the now

famous justice. They sent her a book by D. H. Lawrence and that book did not please her; it brought a blush to her cheek. Very well. But it never occurred to her that there might be people in the world to whom that book might give a high and enlarging pleasure; it never occurred to her that those people had as much right to their pleasure as she had to her blush. So instead of quietly sending the book back for those people to read and getting for herself a nice story by Gene Stratton-Porter, she aroused her father to a state of mind that is increasing the sum of useless folly in the world. People have so little humility, so little goodness. They are so terribly in the right, so rancorously moral. To be saved by them is a proceeding that no person with any kindliness or any spirit could endure.

In some little town or big town of this strange and wonderful country there was recently organized an anti-flirting league and its leaders were duly depicted in the rotogravure supplements of the Sunday newspapers. These ladies and gentlemen were determined that there should be no shy endearments in public parks, no good-night kisses in doorways under the moon, no gazing or touching of hands. They were very stern-looking ladies and gentlemen. We cannot in honesty say that they looked either kind or handsome. We were immensely sure that they didn't flirt with each other and that no one had any designs upon their ferocious delicacy in the matter. The photographs may have done them wrong. But they looked as dour as dungeons and as moral as masonry.

Such has never been the aspect of the great saints or sages who have really bettered the world. It was said of St. Francis that he had the quality of *cortesia*, by which his contemporaries and disciples meant a courtesy of the heart, a profound gentleness, a manly sweetness. Nor is it related of Spinoza that he was noisy in dispute and hoped for a time when his great doctrines would be forced upon others by law. The great truthseekers have always had too much faith in the triumph of truth, the great exemplars of goodness too high a belief in its native and unborrowed persuasiveness to make shrill noises or futile laws or drag their fellows either away from their natural pleasures or to some prison for the body or the mind. Yes, the saints and sages always had the notes of tolerance and gentleness and goodness of heart. Well, that is a lesson which our angry and busy reformers will not learn. Were they capable of learning it they would not be what they are. But when one is tempted to be annoyed by their antics one cannot do better than meditate on the characters and methods of those whose thoughts and teachings have really affected human life. For when one does that, one knows that these reformers are not to be feared; they are rather to be pitied; for it is not comfortable to desire to use force where force is futile and to be self-righteous and right and moral and baffled by what, in such a state of mind, one must necessarily consider the terrible wickedness of a sunless world.

THE AMERICAN NOTE

The Fascist cry of "discipline and hierarchy" versus liberty and spontaneity has found both loud and muffled echoes among us. The name of liberty is still—a mere tradition—upon many lips. But the torch burns low. An evil sophistication tries to identify liberty with the liberty of the sovereign state; let the state be secure and mighty, let the citizen be enslaved. Prohibitions are massed upon prohibitions, censorships upon censorships. The universal darkness of Pope's famous passage is fast coming upon us. In this situation Mr. Stuart Sherman counsels us to cultivate our national past. We shall follow his counsel. Perhaps we shall find in that national past words and voices that he and others of a like temper no longer choose to hear.

That the nation was founded upon the right of revolution is a commonplace. Like many sacred commonplaces it has lost the sting and vitality of truths apparently new. People read the Declaration of Independence and Lincoln's Second Inaugural and hear only well-sounding words. It is not a commonplace that when the nation found its spiritual selfhood, when American voices first proclaimed things American, the doctrine of revolution was transferred from politics to manners and morals, from the affairs of the market-place and the senate to those of the mind and the sovereign will. "I am ashamed to think," wrote Emerson, "how easily we capitulate to badges and names, to large societies and dead institutions." "Institutions," he declared, "are not aboriginal," and "the law is only a memorandum." With the serenest irony he brushed aside those who believe "that any measure, though it were absurd, may be imposed upon a people, if only you can get sufficient voices to make it a law."

Schoolmasters no doubt interpret this as idealistic verbiage. But Emerson went to the last root of this matter. He is as practical a counselor as Jesus. "I do not wish to expiate but to live." And in what manner did he conceive the living of a free, a noble, an American life? "Absolve you to yourself and you shall have the suffrage of the world. . . . What I must do is all that concerns me; not what people think." There is nothing here about teamwork, nothing about rotarianism, nothing about a subservience of poet, seer, or any free man to a Mr. Sumner or a Justice Ford or to a recruiting officer of either the body or the mind.

In Europe, where people have the habit of cultivating their national past, they read Whitman when they desire to be instructed concerning America. They read: "Resist much, obey little;" they read: "I refuse putting from me what I really am;" they read: "I will show that whatever happens to anybody it may be turned to beautiful results," and also: "Do not call the tortoise unworthy because she is not something else." They read these things and call America fortunate, as Goethe did so long ago, because she has moldy citadels neither in her cities nor in her minds but can venture forth upon the great experiment of making human life, freed from an outgrown past, conform to reason and to the spontaneous nature of the race alone.

THE AMERICAN NOTE

The new patriots of criticism are angry at our new poets and novelists. What are these writers doing but echoing creatively that tremendous saying of Thoreau: "The mass of men lead lives of quiet desperation. What is called resignation is confirmed desperation." And Thoreau's way out of this land of desperation was precisely the way out to which our insurgent novelists point. "Man's capacities have never been measured; nor can we judge of what he can do by any precedents, so little has been tried." He did not mean vain inventions. He meant experimenting with life "through obedience to the laws of one's being." "The surface of the earth is soft and impressible by the feet of men; and so with the paths which the mind travels. How worn and dusty, then, must be the highways of the world—how deep the ruts of tradition and conformity." Here again is the American concept of freedom, of independence, which Whitman defined as "freedom from all laws or bonds except those of one's own being controlled by the universal ones."

We have a national past to cultivate, a past dedicated to freedom, to the right of revolution, to the creative life in its widest and fullest sense. We have an American "note," clear, noble, vibrant, the note of all hope for men. That note is in Emerson's "It is the whipper who is whipped, and the tyrant who is undone;" it is in Whitman's "All truths wait in all things;" it is in Thoreau's "The universe is wider than our view of it," a saying matchless but for Goethe's "The world-spirit is more tolerant than we think." Let us dwell upon that note. It will make life more friendly and more beautiful; it will make controversy less acrimonious; it may even Americanize the ignorant and stubborn alien where both the command: "Conform or get out!" and Mr. Brander Matthews's "Poems of American Patriotism" have so dismally failed.

THE AMERICAN NOTE

It is but natural that people should want to be healthy and happy. Most of them would hardly be able to define their notion of what happiness, for themselves, would mean. But they feel aches and lacks and dissatisfactions and confusions, and since they have never been taught that wisdom, which is hard to come by, may help them out, they run after nostrums. This is flat commonplace. It is not without importance to the reflective mind to point out that today, and not by any means in America alone, people run after the same nostrums after which they ran in the years that followed the Thirty Years' War, the same ones that were so popular in the declining years of Rome.

THE HUNT FOR HAPPINESS

The latter parallel is striking and instructive. Occult Eastern rites were brought to Rome; people were healed by magic of all sorts; Isis had her temple in the Eternal City, and the disillusioned matrons of the outworn aristocracy drifted thither for a healing of their largely fancied ills. There was only one whom that world was slow to heed: a pacifist, a non-resister, a good deal of a communist, and a moral revolutionary who swept away all the arguments of the conservatives about saving the state and property and the institutions founded by the fathers, with the simple but ineffably devastating and far-reaching remark that the Sabbath was made for man and not man for the Sabbath. Him the world did not heed until time and tradition and credulity had made of Him, too, a healer, a magician, and a myth.

It is extraordinarily interesting and, to the historical mind, not a little saddening, to watch the religious notices in the New York Sunday press. There is Christian Science, popular, powerful, and almost conservative now. But there is also a "divine science" that competes in the art of healing. And there is, of all grotesque things in the world when you consider the saving intellectualism of the race, a "Jewish Science," and rabbis who preach Sunday sermons on Health and Faith. All these are nothing in their pretensions to what one might call the freelances of the New Healing and the New Thought. There is a lady who calls herself a "curative psychologist and personality builder," and declares that she has helped many to "health, happiness, and success." There is a gentleman who proposes to establish the "volitional empire," a lady who promises to heal you of your habits, a lady and gentleman who teach "healing in the involuntary way." There is still another lady who preaches on How to Get the Things You Want and there are various other "healing services," and "hours of prayer and healing" and lectures on "Stock-Taking for Success." The lady responsible for the latter performance adds with an almost sweet simplicity: "These lectures are helping people in business. They will help you." The Theosophists top off this whole display with their discourses on "psychism, occultism, and magic," their "letters on occultism," and their promise to teach you the "secret doctrine." You glance upward and away from these and you see that, at the Church of the Ascension, the Rev. Dr. Percy Stickney Grant is going to preach on The Immoralities of Religion, and you take heart. But not for long. You may be sure that the conventicles and esoteric lecture halls are crowded with eager seekers, and that the intellectuals who hear Dr. Grant are in substantial agreement with him anyhow. And next some one of whom you had thought better drops in to bore you about Coué. You retire into a corner murmuring: "O miseras hominum mentis, o pectora cæca!" It is cold comfort.

All these people who hunt for happiness want to be saved without being born again. They do not want to change their social habits or views, or to think hard, or to seek for the causes of things, or to undergo the discipline of scientific and philosophical culture. They want to go on living in the economic and social institutions of Main Street and then, by some formula or charm or bit of downright magic, be cured of the ills which those very institutions and the habits bred by those institutions and laws have caused. They want a plaster, but really no cure at all. You will rarely find a true liberal or radical in their ranks. They want war *and* inner peace, sex-slavery *and* harmonious human relations, unbridled capitalism *and* unvarying business success for themselves. Jesus is too radical for them, and Goethe too immoral, and science too upsetting. They want magic and the moon. To understand them thus is perhaps one way of helping them; it is, at least, a safeguard against becoming involved with them oneself.

The intellectuals are not loved in any country. The intellectuals do not love themselves. They are martyrs; they are martyrs to what they themselves have created. Yet they have created it for the good of mankind. Things of use and wisdom are their products. By their efforts man cleaves the air and conquers disease and sees his span of life lengthened and sees order and beauty where chaos prevailed. The creators of these benefits are left isolated, jeered at, outcast, often a weariness to themselves.

For the intellectual remains a man. He has all the biological, all the atavistic urges. He wants the comfort of being at one with his folk, of acting, at times at least, out of folk-instinct, communal passion, of being leader rather than rebel and martyr. It does not, except by an inverted psychical process, really please him to outrage the Philistines, bait the Babbitts, bully the "booberie." How he would like the comforts of neighborliness of the spirit, to drop the wretched veiled condescension forced upon him by his own character in all intercourse but that with his fellows; how, at moments, he needs, in this fundamental and ancient sense, the simple life!

He envies the men of other ages. The subtlest schoolman, the greatest prelate of the Middle Ages did but more thoroughly and completely understand what the clown at his gate and the hind in his fields believed without understanding. Schoolman and cobbler held the same views both physical and metaphysical. They could converse upon a common basis. No gulf of misunderstanding separated them. They could be neighbors and friends.

The twentieth-century intellectual is cut off from communication with his folk. The people still have myth; he has none. The myth may be merely some shabby absolute in questions of conduct and government. It sunders the believer hopelessly from the confirmed relativist. No common ground is left, not common ground enough even for disagreement. When the myths become thick and hot there is no possibility of speech. What will you say to a man who believes in hell, or that the Pope of Rome wants to run this country, or that the Jews caused the war, or that Darwinism is a devilish device to undo the pure in heart, or that the authority of the majority should be absolute, or that want of flat conformity should be penalized by expulsion from the state? How would you argue with a Methodist minister from an Arkansas village, with a Kleagle of the Klan, with a "this-is-a-white-man's country" politician from central Georgia? Nor is this all. Can you contend with a billionaire industrialist who thinks, and avows his thought, that "history is bunk"?

No common speech is left, no common ground. The scientific and philosophical discoveries of the past hundred and fifty years with their accompanying perceptions have caused men who exist simultaneously to live in different ages, ages that have little power of communicating with each other. They have robbed the intellectual of folk, country, tribe, home. When ultimate decisions come he has, in self-defense, to act with his people, even to try to act through them. He cannot be left dangling in the void. But he can never be whole-hearted, never whole-heartedly at one with the mass. He has infinite mental reservations—he is, indeed, a creature of mental reservations—and must first build up a philosophy which will permit him to act with his fellow-men without wholly destroying the honor of his mind.

He is a democrat and fears the power of the democracy, a libertarian who knows that when the people speak of liberty they mean liberty to do the conventional will of any majority in village, county, State, where the test happens to be applied. He is a humanitarian and knows that they who echo his words will always make exceptions that destroy his notion—unbelievers, public enemies, those guilty of sedition. He is passionately loyal to truth. But he cannot display that passion. Heresy-trials are conducted on ostensibly the same principle. He employs all words in special senses, lives in the flowing and creative world whose very existence is hotly denied by every word and act of his fellow-citizens, and finds his final refuge in silence or mild irony.

All the while he suffers, unless he has a divine Miltonic arrogance or a Goethean serenity, from malaise and homelessness. That explains his occasional romantic yearning for Periclean Athens, for mediæval Rome. His golden age is either a past or a Utopia of oneness, union between himself and others, outer harmony and so inner peace. He wavers, in proportion to his vitality, between Novalis and Wells. He is always escaping into past or future. He is pitiable and magnificent, destined to creativeness and gloom, to service and to isolation.

MAN AND FOLK

THE STATESMAN. I recognize your arguments. They are old acquaintances. I not only recognize them; I admit their force. But the problem is salvation, salvation in a temporal sense. That can come only from a deed. We must act.

PHILOSOPHER VS. STATESMAN

THE PHILOSOPHER. There was a thinker once—you've never heard of him—who said that all action is a sign of limitation. Before you act you must exclude all other possible actions. You must almost assert, at least to yourself, the absoluteness of the value of the deed you choose out of all possible deeds.

STATESMAN. That is vicious intellectualism. Every politician is bound to be a pragmatist. The deed to be done is the fruitful deed.

PHILOSOPHER. What a dangerous doctrine!

STATESMAN. It is the only possible one. We cannot stagnate.

PHILOSOPHER. I am not so sure that abstention from action which you call stagnation would not often be fruitful, that saturation with the idea of a situation would not often help to solve it.

STATESMAN. That sounds true. No doubt it is true in the schools. In my life decisions must be made, since all are immediate and final. Every question is a question of life and death—often literally, often for thousands.

PHILOSOPHER *vs.* STATESMAN

PHILOSOPHER. And always for your career.

STATESMAN. Certainly. And it is my clear right to guard my career since its continuance is the condition of my service to men, the condition of causing my ideas, supposing them to have value, to prevail.

PHILOSOPHER. The trouble with your doctrine is its universality of application.

STATESMAN. I thought that was a virtue in every doctrine.

PHILOSOPHER. If the statesman must act and act pragmatically and also save his career in order to make himself—I beg your pardon, his ideas—prevail; if that is all, if you forbid the consideration of truth, you make out a perfect case for any person in power—for Mussolini, for Hitler, for the leader of every red terror, every white terror. Each of them acts out on the instant the pragmatically fruitful truth of his personality and situation. In brief, your doctrine is strictly that old and shoddy one that might is right.

STATESMAN. Not at all.

PHILOSOPHER. We are alone, you know.

STATESMAN. Well, what can a man who has power do but exert that power as seems best to him?

PHILOSOPHER. He can do nothing else indeed. And since it is never a philosopher who is in power——

STATESMAN. Heaven forbid!

PHILOSOPHER. Since, at all events, it never is, the action you defend will always be half-blind because it will always spring from hot convictions, from fear, from opportunism——

STATESMAN. You speak contemptuously of hot convictions. What is nobler?

PHILOSOPHER. The hotter they are, the more ignoble are they likely to be, and the more destructive. Nothing is as sure of itself as ignorance. Isn't that natural? There are no obstacles in its path. Nothing is so sure of itself as fanaticism. Mr. Bryan knows exactly how the world is to be saved; every Kleagle of the Klan knows that too. It's simple. Anatole France is very doubtful; Bertrand Russell hunts for scraps of tentative truth. Action is indeed easy to those who are not fit to act at all.

STATESMAN. You are trying to foist a paradox on me. It follows, I suppose, that those who are worthy of acting cannot and will not and dare not act.

PHILOSOPHER. Precisely. You complete my philosophic truth in its correct form.

STATESMAN. Form?

PHILOSOPHER. Yes. In the world of practice, since there is a world of practice, we cannot indeed adhere to the strict forms of truth.

STATESMAN. Ah, you will become pragmatic in a minute!

PHILOSOPHER. Not at all. What I have said is absolutely and universally true. To translate that truth into action means this: To be afraid of power, to abstain from power as far as is humanly speaking possible, to be afraid of it and abstain from it

PHILOSOPHER vs. STATESMAN

not through personal considerations, but on the ground of the old and precious saying that no man is good enough to rule another.

STATESMAN. And who is then to wield the irreducible minimum of power in society, since there must be such wielding?

PHILOSOPHER. Those who fear power and hate it and take no pride or glory in it, who exercise it after prayers and tears, to whom the wielding of it is sacrifice and bitter service.

STATESMAN. Mystics, then?

PHILOSOPHER. God forbid! The incorruptible intellects who have thought their way clean through to its essential evil. Not statesmen, of all people.

STATESMAN. Nor professional philosophers, I hope.

PHILOSOPHER. I am not so sure. There are philosophers and philosophers.

THE CHEERFUL PESSIMIST

Optimist and pessimist have long ceased to be terms that have any relation to the reason or to the nature of things. The one is supposed simply to cheer, the other to depress the normally aspiring soul, and it is a well-nigh forgotten exercise to examine the grounds of either's private acts or public utterances. Thus it has come to pass that he who in no sense despairs either of the republic or of mankind, but holds the ills of both to be discoverable and remediable, is fitted out by the popular imagination with a forbidding scowl and a poisoned tongue. Your blithe "booster," on the other hand, who keeps smiling according to the almost national slogan and declares that all things work together for the good of the reasonably healthy in body and honest in business is paid a dollar a word for his editorials and reckoned among the Forces for Good.

It is worth while to examine for a moment this man's title to the name of optimist. He does not, in reality, see the best side of things, because his concern is not with things at all. He thinks he can pack away his own troubles and the troubles of the world in his old kit bag and have any reason left for smiling. He forgets that the troubles as well as the heartening things of human life are not accidental but inherent in nature. To pack them away is to leave them untouched and uncured. A man afflicted with some grave disorder may indeed, unless the pain becomes too acute, dismiss the fact from his mind and keep smiling until neither medication nor the surgeon's knife can save him from his fate. He may, during the process, give a fleeting cheer to the unobservant only to shock them the more harrowingly by the apparent suddenness of his taking off. But that man can hardly be thought of as an encouraging or an heroic figure. His course of action has been motivated by a hopelessness of alleviation and a terror of the inexorable truth. He is a vivid symbol of your commoner type of optimist. The cheer he brings is pitiful and brief enough.

We have not yet exhausted his psychology. Beneath his hiding away of his own troubles and the troubles of the world are not only despair and fear; there is the steady though obscure hope of a miracle. In the only kind of a story he will read or play

THE CHEERFUL PESSIMIST

that he will witness, a moral or material miracle, a sudden uncaused change from "bad" to "good," is the central and quite unvarying requirement that he makes. In order to pursue his course and keep his temper he needs constantly to be assured that unexpected inheritances, recoveries of health, and unmotivated changes in human character are part of that disorder which he calls his world. It is, therefore, your professional optimist who fills the coffers of the oil-stock crook, the quack and esoteric healer, the vulgar revivalist. A nation of boosters and smilers supports an unprecedented crowd of miracle-mongers and shies nervously at anyone who tries to strip it of its childish faith in suppressions and palliatives and miracles and lead it toward the tonic world of reality.

Thus it has come about that he who is commonly known among us as a "knocker," a pessimist, and a depressing fellow is nothing in the world but one who has a little courage, a little honest willingness to "face the music," a little hope that things in their real nature are not immedicably foul and wrong. If he fixes his attention upon the darker aspects of reality, it is because these are most to be feared and need, therefore, to be watched in the hope that they may be ameliorated or destroyed. He is often accused because he will not substitute a brand-new panacea for an ancient abuse. But that very unwillingness is a further proof of his fine trust that men can be saved by reason and their own natures and need not necessarily be driven from a crumbling prison into one just built.

For faith in miracles and nostrums our pessimist substitutes a faith in the final manageableness of things. To hope to manage them he must know them as they really are. But this investigation does not depress him in the least. For he is anything but a moral nominalist and he finds much to love and to hope for where the optimist permits himself to be frightened by a bad name. He may not cultivate the perpetual grin, but his gravity will be richly punctuated by laughter; he is no unreflective hustler and booster; he is normally well employed and steadfastly serene. He is amused to think how even Arthur Schopenhauer, the reputed father of his tribe, though he identified the Will to Live with evil in its absolute nature, continued with a passion undiminished by age to proclaim the doctrines he had invented and thus, through a sort of inverted meliorism, bore witness to his faith that a discoverable truth will yet save mankind and make it free. THE CHEERFUL PESSIMIST

In every age the comfortable citizen takes fright and becomes indignant over ideas which seem to threaten the comfort of his mind or the stability of his possessions. Since it does not please him to ascribe these ideas to the necessary processes of thought, he derives them from the evil machinations of tribal or racial aliens and takes satisfaction in damning, at various times, the revolutionists of France, the thinkers of Germany, the communists of Russia, and, when all else fails, the conspiracies of Israel. If he but knew a little more he could THE RED THREAD be more fatalistic but also more cheerful. The ideas that he dreads are almost as old as the history of thinking man; yet their translation into action has been both gradual and fitful. The majority does indeed rule and he and his kind seem in no danger of losing their supreme advantage. Had Mr. Bryan read Lucretius he would be calmer; a pleasing quiet would steal into the hearts of the pleaders for propriety in a thousand pulpits did they but know how little mankind has heeded the instructions concerning love which the wise prophetess Diotima gave Socrates so many centuries ago.

But let us leave both the ancient and the alien and pick up the red thread of revolutionary ideas within the safe and proper field of our own civilization. Every schoolboy knows the essays of Francis Bacon; he also has it, on Macaulay's authority, that Bacon was a great thinker but a bad man. What neither he nor his elders know is the "Novum Organum." "It is idle," Bacon wrote there, "to expect any great advancement in science from the superinducing or engrafting of new things upon old. We must begin anew from the very foundations unless we would revolve forever in a circle of mean and contemptible progress." "Ah," comes the reply, "but he meant physics and geography." Listen a moment more to the old radical: "Men must force themselves to lay their notions by and begin to familiarize themselves with facts." The reddest "red" asks no more than that! Nor could he give a more stinging account of all he repudiates than Bacon did for him. "All the received systems are but so many stage-plays, representing worlds of their own creation after an unreal and scenic fashion." Nor must one comfortably suppose these old giants to have been unpractical or unwilling to touch, if they had had the means, the structure of society. A hundred years before the "Novum Organum" appeared, Sir Thomas More in the second book of his "Utopia," in an astonishing section called "Of Science, Crafts, and Occupations," passionately advocated the universal obligation of productive labor and the six-hour working day. Twenty years after the "Novum Organum," again, John Milton on the floor of the Puritan Parliament thundered against a censorship of the arts with a fire and magnificence that are far to seek today and with grim humor—"lest I should be condemned of introducing licence, while I oppose licensing"—thought to demolish finally the arguments that seem to many at this moment as new as a new-cut tooth.

These things are known to few. Even when they are known the knowledge remains vague and academic and the documents are used in the schools not as records of experience but as exercises in style. Teachers and pupils both desire, first of all, to be comfortable. They need only their own instincts and not the grave John Locke to tell them that "man is not permitted without censure to follow his own thoughts in the search of truth, when they lead him ever so little out of the common road." Thus after nearly two centuries and a half since Locke finally settled the question in the third chapter of the "Essay on the Human Understanding," to assert the relativity of moral values is still indignantly held to be the chief of heresies.

The work of the Renaissance, in other words, far from being completed, has scarcely been begun. At the time of the French Revolution it had its hour of acceleration. Then a new and deeper hush prevailed. What pacifist has gone beyond the boy Shelley? "Man has no right to kill his brother. It is no excuse that he does so in uniform: he only adds the infamy of servitude to the crime of murder." What economic rebel has stated the fundamentals more clearly than he? "No man has a right to monopolize more than he can enjoy; what the rich give to the poor is not a perfect favor but an imperfect right." Is it any wonder that conservatives carefully built up the legend that Shelley was a divine poet but an irresponsible fool? To hear the preceptist critics you would think that Hazlitt had never written, to hear American democrats in solid clubs that neither Lincoln nor Whitman had ever lived. No, nothing is more difficult than to persuade men "to lay their notions by and begin to familiarize themselves with facts!" Yet what a healing process that would be! It would enlighten a few; it would rob the many of that terror in the name of which they persecute and torment as wicked innovators those who but revive the half-forgotten wisdom of the race.

EPILOGUE

FROM the "Sprüche in Versen," the "Sprüche in Prosa," from hundreds of passages scattered up and down the vast correspondence as well as from a few formal essays it is possible and, in truth, not difficult to state once more the critical attitude and philosophy that has caused men as different as Sainte-Beuve and Matthew Arnold, Remy de Gourmont and John Morley to pronounce Goethe the supreme critic of all times.

That critical philosophy may be quite briefly formulated: (1) Art is personal and creates its own laws by what it is; (2) art is the expression of concrete experience; (3) the concretely real is the universally significant.

In his twenty-fourth year Goethe had completely thought out the liberation of the artist from the preceptists of his century. "More harmful to the genius than examples are rules." He addresses the entire progeny of Boileau: "You wish to teach us what we ought to use since what we do use cannot be justified according to your principles." The year of that remark was 1773. It is not superfluous yet. The desire to systematize the universe once and for all and to force art to illustrate your little pet systematization of it has not yet fled the critical breast. In 1799 Goethe summed up the matter in final form: "Art itself gives laws." And by that he meant not that the art of the ancients or of some "grand siècle" gives laws to the artists that follow, but that each genuine creative work comes into being according to an inner law of its own which is completely stated only when that work is itself complete. From this truth arises the psychological corollary that "every artistic production places us in the same state of mind in which the author was." From it arises as well the necessary method of the critic, which is to ask: "What did the author set out to do? Was his plan reasonable and sensible, and how far did he succeed in carrying it out?" And from it finally arises the critical mood which is one of "wise passiveness" and sympathetic receptivity: "If you read a book and let it work upon you, and yield yourself up entirely to its influence, then, and only then, will you arrive at a correct judgment of it."

It was from Goethe the poet that Goethe the critic learned to know the fundamental nature of art as the expression of experience. All his poems were, in the deepest sense, "poems of occasion"— *Gelegenheitsgedichte*. Without the *Gelegenheit* in reality there could be no creation in art. "I have never uttered anything which I have not experienced and which has not urged me to production. I have only composed love songs when I have loved. How could I write songs of hatred without hating?" And what applied to the simplest lyric he knew how to apply with equal force to the most elaborate works of the creative imagination. Hence he saw clearly that reality is the soil of art and that "at bottom no real object is unpoetical, if the poet knows how to treat it properly." The denial of *a priori* unpoeticalness as inherent in any reality makes Goethe the prophetic and magnificent liberator of all art since his time.

He knew of course that expression must be communication, that the concrete experience of the poet must speak to all men. But he saw at once that, from the very nature of things, such was indeed the case. "A particular case becomes universal and poetic by the very circumstance that it is treated by a poet." And not by that circumstance alone. He had learned from Spinoza that the qualities of a thing are of its essence; therefore the essence of any thing—any *ens*—is of the essence of the universe itself and therefore of the essence of God. Thus he knew it to be as true philosophically as practically that "if a thing be but well represented in art it will symbolize all else" and serenely pronounced his ultimate critical maxim which applies to nature as well as to art:

> Willst du ins Unendliche schreiten,
> Geh nur im Endlichen nach allen Seiten.

The measure in which the artistic projection of concrete experience becomes universal is the measure of the poet's creative power. It is "according to his powers" that "each one is able to develop the uni-

GOETHE THE CRITIC

versal out of a special case." But the process is a natural one and conformable to the character of man and of his world in which all the perishable things are also imperishable because they are symbols. "Alles Vergängliche ist nur ein Gleichnis." But by virtue of being not only but necessarily symbols of eternal things the concrete experiences of mortality assume a supreme importance. Thus our passions are justified; our pangs are part of a lasting order; our art, founded in the soil of life, to the extent in truth to which it is deeply founded therein, is touched, like a tall, deep-rooted tree, by the light of a sun that does not set or darken.

GOETHE AND OURSELVES

It was the late Professor Hume Brown who called Goethe "one of the supreme councilors of humanity." And it is in the origin and nature of his council to mankind that the supreme significance and fascination of Goethe lie. The beauty that he brings us is not remote or enshrined or transmuted, prior to its expression, into some cultural tradition or formal medium that time is beginning to tarnish. All the other great poets lived in a fixed and finished world, in a cosmic or a moral system in which the fate of every action and quality was assumed to be foreknown. Goethe was the first realist in the modern sense, and he is still the greatest. He surveyed himself and mankind and human life not under the guidance of pre-established ideas, but as they are in their own nature and in their native significance and beauty. He created ideas in life and vision in art through passion and action themselves, and his ultimate counsel of dying to live—"Stirb und werde"—is the exact contrary of the Pauline monition in that it means not the elimination but the absorption and transcendence of experience. To put the matter very simply, if you would avoid drowning, don't flee the water but learn to swim.

We must, in a word, strive onward with the universe which is not only a being but a becoming, not a mere static spectacle but a procession in which our road is also our goal. It is

> Gestaltung, Umgestaltung,
> Des ewigen Sinnes ewige Unterhaltung.

Men differ from each other; man differs from himself.

> Der Mensch ist ungleich, ungleich sind die Stunden.

Long before Nietzsche or the modern sociologists Goethe knew that man creates false moral absolutes out of his own narrow and special propensities and that thus each one

> das Beste was er kennt,
> Er Gott, ja seinen Gott benennt.

Therefore he issues the broad command of tolerance:

> Tu, was du willst, nur habe nicht recht.

And therefore in a universe of relativity he substitutes the concept of error for that of sin and the concept of creative self-direction for that of conformity to the unreal absolutes of a rigid system. "The world spirit," he declared, "is far more tolerant than people think." And hence he held it to be quaint and amusing that among men "each grudges the other the right to err in his fashion." He made the sharpest differentiation between mere whim and the command of the inner law and was under no illusion as to the difficulty of our mortal conflicts:

> Wer nicht verzweifeln kann, der muss nicht leben.

But he repudiated all forms of external moral or intellectual compulsion: "Wandle doch jeder nach seiner Art"; he repudiated all fugitive and cloistered virtues and felt life to be, upon these terms, an heroic creative adventure:

> Lasst mich nur auf meinem Sattel gelten!
> Bleibt in euren Hütten, euren Zelten!
> Und ich reite froh in alle Ferne,
> Ueber meiner Mütze nur die Sterne!

He felt it to be, above all, a cosmic adventure. He lived wholly in the concrete, yet wholly in the infinite, too. God moves the universe from within even as man "lives from within outward," and nature has "neither kernel nor shell." Thus Goethe destroyed the false distinction between a variable earthly and an unvarying eternal order and lived at every moment within that process of creative change which is the universe. "I know no other aim," he wrote, "than to realize myself, in my own way, as far as possible, in order that I may partake of this infinite in which we are placed in an ever happier and purer way."

Toward his views and toward his example all

modern philosophy and all modern science converge. The masses of mankind are still engulfed in futile conflict and intolerance. But wherever the modern mind attains its highest and clearest consciousness, whether through poetry or philosophy or science, it finds its ultimate conclusions foretold and expressed by Goethe. Therefore his sayings and gnomic poems, his letters and conversations and "Faust"—the entire poem, of course, and not merely the Gretchen tragedy—are the true books of wisdom of this age, and his life is the great exemplar toward which many strive darkly and many with all possible vigilance of soul. For that life was truly self-governed, tolerant, whole, and free. It transmuted passion into vision and business into wisdom; it steeped itself in the concrete and found the universal there; it achieved the triumph of personality within the cosmic flux and came upon all aspects of the eternal in the necessary employments of our human day.

> Whether day my spirit's yearning
> Unto far, blue hills has led,
> Or the night lit all the burning
> Constellations at my head—
> Hours of light or hours nocturnal
> Do I praise our mortal fate:
> If man think the thought eternal
> He is ever fair and great.